snacks

Whole-wheat focaccia
with rosemary, p. 122

Salmon carpaccio with lemon
& peppercorns, p. 148

Brie & peach tartlets,
p. 60

Lemon tartlets p. 300

Tuscan chicken liver crostini,
p. 54

Shrimp skewers, p. 172

Oregano breadsticks, p. 72

Peanut brittle, p. 314

Beet dip with toast, p. 22

MARINA NERI

snacks

DELICIOUS RECIPES FOR A HEALTHY LIFE

Reader's Digest

THE READER'S DIGEST ASSOCIATION, INC.
New York, New York / Montreal / Singapore

A READER'S DIGEST BOOK
This edition published by
The Reader's Digest Association, Inc.
by arrangement with McRae Publishing Ltd

Publishers: Anne McRae, Marco Nardi
Project Director Anne McRae
Art Director Marco Nardi
Photography R&R Photostudio, Brent Parker Jones
Text Marina Neri
Editing Foreign Concept
Food Styling Lee Blaylock
Layouts Filippo Delle Monache
Prepress Filippo Delle Monache

ISBN 978-1-55475-130-3

For more Reader's Digest products and information, visit our websites:
   www.rd.com (in the United States)
   www.readersdigest.ca (in Canada)
   www.rdasia.com (in Asia)
   www.readersdigest.com.au (in Australia)

Printed in China

NOTE TO OUR READERS
Eating eggs or egg whites that are not completely cooked poses the possibility of salmonella food poisoning. The risk is greater for pregnant women, the elderly, the very young, and persons with impaired immune systems. If you are concerned about salmonella, you can use reconstituted powdered egg whites or pasteurized eggs.

Contents

Introduction 10

Choosing a Snack 12

Crostini, Canapés & Dips 16

Bready Things 66

Fishy Fun 136

Meat & Chicken Bites 178

Garden Fresh 220

Something Sweet 282

Index 316

Introduction

The key to a healthy diet lies in serving food freshly prepared at home using high quality ingredients. This is especially true when it comes to snack food. Our supermarkets are overflowing with pre-packaged snacks that are mass-produced using low-quality ingredients and preservatives and packed with too many unhealthy sugars and fats. Vending machines in schools and many other public places along with fast-food outlets on every street corner, only add to the problem.

Here you will find more than 140 recipes for a wide range of snacks, from crostini and breads to fish, meat, and vegetable dishes. We have also included a chapter of sweet snacks to finish. With this book you can plan ahead, making sure that your family and friends enjoy only the best.

You will notice that we have included some fried dishes and others that are rich in butter and sugar. We don't think you should serve these snacks every day; but on special occasions a fried tidbit or a square of fudge can be enjoyed without spoiling an overall healthy diet.

Enjoy!

SYMBOLS		
	Serves 4–6	**Serves** The number of portions
	30 minutes	**Preparation** Time to prepare the dish, excluding cooking & resting
	1 hour	**Chilling & Resting** "Down time" when dish is chilling, resting, etc
These symbols are used throughout the book. They mean:	15 minutes	**Cooking** Cooking time
	2	**Difficulty** From 1 (easy) to 3 (challenging). Most recipes are 1 or 2

opposite: pretzels, p. 68

choosing a snack

This book has more than 140 recipes for mouthwatering snacks—something for everyone, and every occasion. But, what if you are not an experienced cook or have just a handful of ingredients in the refrigerator? The EASY section below will solve the first problem and the JUST A FEW INGREDIENTS on page 14 will solve the second. Looking for an old favorite? See our CLASSICS suggestions. See also the VEGETARIAN, HEALTHY CHOICE, and EDITOR'S CHOICE recommendations.

EASY

quick cheese & onion bread, p. 130

crab & avocado salad, p. 140

tuna & pickles crostini, p. 42

quick savory loaf, p. 132

meatballs with sage butter, p. 216

classic beef burgers, p. 192

salami with fresh figs, p. 180

VEGETARIAN

gorgonzola & onion pizza with fresh sage, p. 110

zucchini flower & rice tartlets, p. 250

tomato sorbet, p. 222

fried mozzarella, p. 280

cheese & celery snacks p. 224

CHALLENGING

petits-fours, p. 306

filled pizzas with tomato & parmesan, p. 106

spinach strudel with fruit chutney p. 260

stuffed rice croquettes, p. 200

stuffed fried olives p. 182

JUST A FEW INGREDIENTS

tuscan bruschetta fingers,
p. 32

prosciutto, peach & blue
cheese crostini, p. 40

palmiers with pine nuts & parmesan, p. 78

tomato & pesto puff
p. 262

strawberry & champagne
granita, p. 284

HEALTHY CHOICE

seafood salad p. 144

smoked salmon dip, p. 28

quick whole-wheat yogurt
bread p. 128

summer potato salad,
p. 232

kiwi sorbet, p. 286

CLASSICS

chocolate truffles p. 308

hummus with toasted focaccia p.18

pretzels, p. 68

beef fajitas, p. 190

chocolate walnut fudge p. 312

EDITOR'S CHOICE

pear & hazelnut crostoni, p. 34

cheese & tomato pinwheels, p. 114

herb tempura, p. 264

roasted bell peppers with anchovies, p. 238

liver pâté, p. 208

leek & almond quiches, p. 254

chocolate macadamia cupcakes, p. 294

Crostini, Canapés & Dips

hummus with toasted focaccia

Hummus is a classic Middle Eastern dish and makes a healthy snack. Tahini is a paste made from crushed sesame seeds. Buy it wherever Middle Eastern foods are sold. Hummus can be served with crudités, crackers, or focaccia. Try it with our recipe for oregano breadsticks (see page 72) or whole-wheat focaccia with rosemary (see page 122).

Serves 4

10 minutes

5 minutes

1

1   (14-ounce/400-g) can garbanzo beans (chickpeas), drained, with 3 tablespoons of the liquid reserved
2   cloves garlic, chopped

3   tablespoons freshly squeezed lemon juice
1/4   cup (60 ml) tahini
4–6   slices sesame or plain focaccia

1. **Preheat** the oven to 350°F (180°C/gas 4). Place the focaccia on a baking sheet and toast for 5 minutes, until warmed through and golden brown.

2. **While the focaccia is toasting,** chop the garbanzo beans and reserved liquid, garlic, lemon juice, and tahini in a food processor. Blend until smooth and well combined.

3. **Put** the hummus in a small serving bowl. Serve with the warm toasted focaccia.

If you liked this recipe, you will love these ones too:

ricotta dip **with crudités**
20

beet dip **with toast**
22

garbanzo bean dip with crudités
24

ricotta dip with crudités

Ricotta is a fresh Italian cheese made from the whey of sheep or cow's milk. It is a good source of protein, calcium, and selenium.

Serves 6

30 minutes

20–30 minutes

3–5 minutes

1

4	scallions (spring onions), trimmed
1	small cauliflower, cut into florets
4	stalks celery
8	baby zucchini (courgettes)
12	radishes
2	small sweet red onions
2	small heads red radicchio
	Pinch of saffron threads
2	tablespoons freshly squeezed lemon juice

1	tablespoon prepared horseradish
	Salt and freshly ground black pepper
⅓	cup (90 ml) extra-virgin olive oil
1	cup (250 g) fresh ricotta cheese, drained
4	tablespoons blanched pistachios, chopped

1. Cut each scallion from the middle, sliding the knife toward the greener end. Repeat this cut several times on each scallion and then place in a bowl of iced water. Let rest until the sliced ends curl, 20–30 minutes. Drain well.

2. Cook the cauliflower in a large pot of salted boiling water until just tender, 3–5 minutes. Drain well and let cool.

3. Slice the celery, zucchini, and radishes into batons or sticks. Slice the onions into rings. Tear the radicchio into manageable pieces.

4. Arrange the prepared vegetables on a large serving dish.

5. Combine the saffron, lemon juice, and horseradish in a small bowl. Season with salt and pepper. Add the oil and ricotta and beat until all the ingredients are well mixed. Stir in the pistachios.

6. Place the bowl of dip on the serving dish with the vegetables and serve.

If you liked this recipe, you will love these ones too:

garbanzo bean dip with crudités

24

tomato & almond pesto

26

baby focaccias with cream cheese & prosciutto

96

beet dip with toast

Dark red beets will stain your hands if you peel them without gloves. You can remove the stains by slicing a potato in half and rubbing it over the stains under cold running water.

Serves 4

15 minutes

30 minutes

45 minutes

1

3 medium (about 1 pound/ 500 g) beets (beetroot/red beet), trimmed

¾ cup (200 g) plain yogurt

2 tablespoons freshly squeezed lemon juice

1 teaspoon ground cumin
Thinly sliced toast or bagel chips, to serve

1. Cook the beets in a large saucepan of boiling water until tender, about 45 minutes. Drain well and set aside for 30 minutes to cool.

2. Peel the beets and coarsely chop. Place in a food processor with the yogurt, lemon juice, and cumin. Blend until smooth and well combined.

3. Transfer the beet dip to a serving bowl. Serve with toast or bagel chips.

If you liked this recipe, you will love these ones too:

hummus with toasted focaccia

smoked salmon dip

taramasalata

18

28

30

garbanzo bean dip with crudités

This delicious dip comes from Morocco where it is known as Bessara. It goes beautifully with sliced raw vegetables, but also with pieces of pita bread or focaccia.

Serves 8–12

15 minutes

12 hours

65 minutes

1

1	pound (500 g) garbanzo beans (chickpeas) or dried fava (broad) beans, soaked overnight and drained
6	cups (1.5 liters) water
4	cloves garlic
1	onion, diced
	Salt
½	cup (125 ml) extra-virgin

	olive oil
2	teaspoons ground cumin
2	teaspoons hot paprika + extra, to dust
	Snipped chives, to garnish
	Raw vegetables, such as celery and carrots, to serve

1. **Place** the garbanzo beans in a large saucepan with the water, garlic, and onion. Bring to a boil and simmer until the beans are very soft, about 1 hour.

2. **Transfer** the beans, garlic, and onion to a food processor and purée until smooth, adding enough of the cooking water to make a smooth, thick dip.

3. **Return** the mixture to the saucepan. Season with salt and stir in the oil, cumin, and paprika. Simmer over low heat until warm, about 5 minutes. Add more cooking liquid if it is too thick.

4. **Pour** into small bowls and garnish with the paprika and chives. Serve as a dip with raw vegetables.

If you liked this recipe, you will love these ones too:

hummus **with toasted focaccia**

18

ricotta dip **with crudités**

20

tomato & almond pesto

If you enjoy the intense tomato flavor of sun-dried tomatoes you will love this pesto.
It also goes well on freshly cooked pasta or rice.

Serves 4–6

10 minutes

1

4	ounces (125 g) sun-dried tomatoes, preserved in oil, drained
½	cup (50 g) whole almonds, toasted
½	cup (25 g) fresh basil leaves
½	cup (25 g) fresh parsley leaves
4	tablespoons freshly grated Parmesan cheese

1	clove garlic
	Salt and freshly ground black pepper
½	cup (125 ml) extra-virgin olive oil
	Storebought or homemade breadsticks (see page 72) or sliced raw vegetables, to serve

1. **Put** the sun-dried tomatoes in a food processor and blend until coarsely chopped. Add the almonds, basil, parsley, Parmesan, and garlic. Season with salt and pepper and, with the machine running, begin gradually adding the oil. This pesto is best with a bit of texture to it, so don't grind the nuts too finely.

2. **Serve** with the breadsticks or vegetables, or both.

If you liked this recipe, you will love these ones too:

beet dip **with toast**

22

garbanzo bean dip with crudités

24

smoked salmon dip

Serve this dip with predinner drinks. It is great with thin, crisp crackers but can also be served with potato chips (crisps), corn chips, or thin slices of toasted bread.

Serves 4

10 minutes

2 hours

1

5	ounces (150 g) smoked salmon (or smoked trout)
1	cup (250 g) light cream cheese, at room temperature
2	tablespoons freshly squeezed lemon juice
1½	tablespoons salt-cured capers, rinsed

2	tablespoons finely chopped fresh dill + a sprig, to garnish
	Salt and freshly ground black pepper
	Crackers, to serve

1. **Process** the smoked salmon, cream cheese, lemon juice, capers, and chopped dill in a food processor until smooth. Season with salt and pepper. Chill in the refrigerator for 2 hours.

2. **Spoon** the dip into a serving bowl, garnish with the sprig of dill, and serve with crackers.

If you liked this recipe, you will love these ones too:

taramasalata

30

smoked salmon rolls with goat cheese

44

simple smoked salmon snack

46

taramasalata

Taramasalata, or cod roe dip, is a classic Greek appetizer. Serve it with crackers and sliced vegetables with predinner drinks, or as part of a spread of eye-catching meze at the beginning of a meal. Look for the fish roe, sometimes called "tarama," wherever Greek foods are sold.

Serves 6–8

15 minutes

2 hours

10–15 minutes

1

2	medium potatoes, peeled and cut into 2–3 pieces
5	ounces (150 g) cod roe or carp roe
1	small onion, finely chopped
2/3	cup (150 ml) extra-virgin olive oil

Freshly squeezed juice of 1 lemon

Salt and freshly ground black pepper

Black olives, to serve

Pita bread, to serve

1. **Cook** the potatoes in a small saucepan of lightly salted boiling water until tender, 10–15 minutes.

2. **Combine** the potatoes, roe, onion, oil, and lemon juice in a food processor and pulse until smooth. Add more oil if the dip is too thick. Season with salt and pepper.

3. **Transfer** to a serving bowl, cover with plastic wrap (cling film), and chill for at least 2 hours before serving.

4. **Serve** with the olives and pita bread.

If you liked this recipe, you will love these ones too:

smoked salmon **dip**

28

tuna & pickles **crostini**

42

seafood bruschetta

50

tuscan bruschetta fingers

Simple almost to the point of austerity, this is a typical Tuscan dish. Be warned though, like all Tuscan food, it will only work if you use the finest ingredients. The oil should be fresh, cold-pressed extra-virgin and the bread should be firmed-textured and preferably unsalted.

Serves 6–8

5 minutes

5–7 minutes

1

8	slices firm-textured white bread, $\frac{1}{2}$ inch (1 cm) thick
2	large cloves garlic
	Salt and freshly ground black pepper
$\frac{1}{2}$	cup (125 ml) extra-virgin olive oil

1. **Preheat** the oven to 400°F (200°C/ gas 6).

2. **Toast** the bread for 5–7 minutes, or until crisp and pale golden brown. It is important that the bread dries out while toasting, which it won't if browned in a toaster. Rub each slice all over with the garlic.

3. **Arrange** the toasted bread on a serving platter. Season with salt and pepper and drizzle with the oil. Cut each slice into 3–4 fingers or squares. Serve warm.

If you liked this recipe, you will love these ones too:

pear & hazelnut **crostoni**

34

crostini **with ratatouille**

36

porcini mushroom **crostini**

38

pear & hazelnut crostoni

You can use any homestyle white or whole-wheat (wholemeal) bread for this recipe. Even a whole-grain or multi-cereal bread will work well because the cheese topping has a strong flavor and will not be overpowered by the bread.

Serves 4

25 minutes

15 minutes

1

3	tablespoons butter
1	shallot, finely chopped
2	large ripe pears, peeled, cored, and sliced
1/4	cup (60 ml) sweet white wine
1/2	teaspoon ground cinnamon
8	slices firm-textured bread

8	ounces (250 g) brie, sliced
	Freshly ground black pepper
1	tablespoon coarsely chopped fresh flat-leaf parsley
2/3	cup (75 g) chopped hazelnuts

1. **Preheat** an overhead broiler (grill) on a high setting.

2. **Melt** the butter in a frying pan over medium heat. Add the shallot and sauté until translucent, 3–4 minutes. Set aside.

3. **Add** the pear to the frying pan and sauté for 2 minutes.

4. **Add** the wine and simmer until it evaporates, about 1 minute.

5. **Remove** from the heat and drain the pears on paper towels. Dust with the cinnamon and let cool slightly.

6. **Toast** the bread under the broiler until golden brown. Lay the brie on the toasted bread.

7. **Add** a layer of shallots and a layer of pear. Broil until the cheese is melted, 2–3 minutes. Season with pepper. Sprinkle with the parsley and hazelnuts. Serve hot.

If you liked this recipe, you will love these ones too:

crostini with ratatouille

36

prosciutto, peach & blue cheese crostini

40

italian sausage crostini

52

crostini with ratatouille

Ratatouille is a delicious vegetable stew originally from Provence in the south of France. It is made with any combination of onion, tomatoes, eggplant, bell pepper, zucchini, and garlic, usually with plenty of fresh herbs such as basil and parsley.

Serves 4

15–20 minutes

30 minutes

1

4	tablespoons (60 ml) extra-virgin olive oil		2	ripe tomatoes, chopped
1	onion, finely chopped			Salt and freshly ground black pepper
1	leek, finely chopped		2	tablespoons coarsely chopped fresh basil
2	zucchini (courgettes), cut into small cubes		8	thick slices firm-textured (homestyle) bread
1	red bell pepper (capsicum), seeded, cored, and cut into small cubes		2	cloves garlic, peeled
1	small eggplant (aubergine), with skin, cut into small cubes			

1. **Heat** 2 tablespoons of oil in a medium saucepan over medium heat.

2. **Add** the onion and leek and sauté until softened, 3–4 minutes. Add the zucchini, bell pepper, eggplant, and tomatoes.

3. **Season** with salt and pepper and simmer until the vegetables are tender, about 25 minutes. Stir in the basil.

4. **While the vegetables are simmering,** toast the bread and rub each slice with garlic. Drizzle with the remaining 2 tablespoons of oil and season lightly with salt.

5. **Spoon** the ratatouille over the crostini and serve warm.

If you liked this recipe, you will love these ones too:

prosciutto, peach & blue cheese **crostini**

40

italian sausage **crostini**

52

tuscan chicken liver **crostini**

54

porcini mushroom crostini

Porcini mushrooms (*boletus edulis*), also known as ceps, grow wild in forests in many parts of the Northern Hemisphere in the fall. If you can't find them fresh for this recipe, use the same amount of cultivated white mushrooms and add 1 ounce (30 g) of reconstituted dried porcinis.

Serves 8–10

20 minutes

25 minutes

1

1 ¼ pounds (600 g) porcini mushrooms
¼ cup (60 ml) extra-virgin olive oil
2 tablespoons butter
1 small onion, finely chopped
2 cloves garlic, finely chopped
1 tablespoon finely chopped fresh thyme + extra sprigs, to garnish

Salt and freshly ground black pepper
½ cup (125 ml) vegetable stock
1 baguette (French loaf), sliced

1. Preheat the oven to 350°F (180°C/gas 4).

2. Separate the stalks from the caps of the mushrooms. Dice the firm unblemished parts of the stalks. Chop the caps coarsely.

3. Heat the oil and butter in a large frying pan over medium heat. Add the onion, garlic, and chopped thyme and sauté until softened, 3–4 minutes.

4. Add the mushrooms and season with salt and pepper. Sauté for 5 minutes.

Gradually stir in enough stock to keep the mixture moist but not sloppy. Simmer over low heat for 8–10 minutes.

5. Spread the bread out on a baking sheet and bake in the oven for about 5 minutes, until crisp and pale golden brown.

6. Spread each crostino with a generous helping of the mushroom mixture. Garnish with the extra sprigs of thyme and serve warm.

If you liked this recipe, you will love these ones too:

pear & hazelnut **crostoni**

34

fried polenta **with mushrooms, peas & cheese**

56

fried polenta pieces **with mushroom sauce**

58

prosciutto, peach
& blue cheese crostini

This is a quick and easy snack to make. If preferred, replace the peach with thin slices of fresh cantaloupe (rockmelon).

Serves 4–6

10 minutes

5 minutes

1

1	baguette (French loaf), thinly sliced on the diagonal
5	ounces (150 g) blue cheese
8	large thin slices prosciutto, (about 4 ounces/120 g), cut in half

2	medium ripe peaches, peeled, pitted, and sliced

1. **Preheat** the oven to 350°F (180°C/ gas 4).

2. **Spread** the bread out on a baking sheet and bake in the oven for about 5 minutes, until crisp and pale golden brown.

3. **Spread** a little cheese on each slice of toast. Fold a half slice of prosciutto on top and cover with a slice of peach. If necessary, hold the topping in place with a toothpick.

4. **Serve** while the toast is still warm.

If you liked this recipe, you will love these ones too:

tuscan **bruschetta fingers**

32

pear & hazelnut **crostoni**

34

brie & peach tartlets

60

tuna & pickles crostini

You can whip this snack up in just a few minutes. If liked, toast the bread in the oven for 5 minutes until crisp and golden brown before spreading with the tuna paste.

Serves 6–8

10 minutes

1

8	ounces (250 g) canned tuna, drained
3	ounces (90 g) cocktail onions
3	ounces (90 g) mixed pickled vegetables, drained

¾	cup (200 ml) mayonnaise
1	baguette (French loaf), sliced

1. **Place** the tuna, cocktail onions, pickled vegetables, and mayonnaise in a blender or food processor.

2. **Process** until finely blended into a smooth paste.

3. **Spread** the paste evenly over the bread. Transfer to a serving plate and serve.

If you liked this recipe, you will love these ones too:

taramasalata
30

smoked salmon rolls **with goat cheese**
44

clam crostini
48

smoked salmon rolls
with goat cheese

Choose small, soft, brioche-style or milk bread rolls for this snack.

Serves 6–8

15 minutes

1

12	mini bread rolls
¾	cup (180 g) soft fresh goat cheese, such as chèvre or caprino, softened
4	tablespoons cream cheese, softened
1	tablespoon finely chopped fresh parsley
2	teaspoons snipped fresh chives
2	tablespoons extra-virgin olive oil
	Freshly ground black pepper
8	ounces (250 g) smoked salmon

1. **Cut** the rolls in half and remove some of the soft part from inside.

2. **Use** a fork to beat the goat cheese and cream cheese in a small bowl.

3. **Mix** in the parsley, chives, and oil. Season with pepper.

4. **Spread** the rolls with the cheese mixture and cover with a slice of smoked salmon. Serve at once.

If you liked this recipe, you will love these ones too:

smoked salmon **dip**

28

simple smoked salmon **snack**

46

seafood **bruschetta**

50

simple smoked salmon snack

This snack is so easy to prepare you won't believe how good it tastes. It is also elegant and can be served with drinks before dinner or as an appetizer for a smart dinner party. Prepare in advance and store in the refrigerator until ready to serve.

Serves 4–6

5 minutes

1

1	multigrain baguette (French loaf), sliced	3	ounces (90 g) salted butter, softened
6	ounces (180 g) best-quality wild smoked salmon, cut into pieces about the size of the slices of bread	2	limes Freshly ground black pepper

1. **Spread** the slices of baguette with the butter. Place a slice of wild salmon on each slice of bread. Drizzle with lime juice, season generously with pepper, and serve.

If you liked this recipe, you will love these ones too:

smoked salmon **dip**

28

smoked salmon rolls **with goat cheese**

44

clam crostini

48

clam crostini

Low in fat and rich in omega-3 fatty acids, clams are a heart-healthy food. They are also a good source of protein, phosphorous, iron, potassium, and vitamin A.

- Serves 8
- 30 minutes
- 1 hour
- 20–25 minutes
- 2

2	pounds (1 kg) clams, in shell
4	tablespoons (60 ml) extra-virgin olive oil
3	cloves garlic, 1 whole, 2 finely chopped
1/2	cup (125 ml) dry white wine
3	tablespoons finely chopped fresh parsley

1–2	dried red chiles, crumbled
2–3	tomatoes, chopped
	Salt
16	slices firm-textured (homestyle) bread

1. **Soak** the clams in a bowl of cold water for 1 hour. Drain well.

2. **Preheat** the oven to 350°F (180°C/gas 4).

3. **Place** the clams, 2 tablespoons of oil, and the whole clove of garlic in a large frying pan over medium-high heat. Pour in the wine, cover the pan, and simmer until the clams have opened, 5–7 minutes. Remove the clams from the frying pan, discarding any that have not opened.

4. **Extract** the clams from the open shells and place in a dish. Cover with a plate so they do not dry out too much.

5. **Heat** the remaining 2 tablespoons of oil in a medium frying pan over medium heat. Add the finely chopped garlic, parsley, and chiles and sauté until the garlic is pale gold, 3–4 minutes.

6. **Add** the tomatoes and season with salt. Simmer until the sauce has reduced, about 10 minutes.

7. **Spread** the bread out on a baking sheet and bake in the oven for about 5 minutes, until crisp and pale golden brown.

8. **Add** the clams to the tomato mixture, stir well, and remove from the heat. Spread over the toasted bread and serve warm.

If you liked this recipe, you will love these ones too:

tuna & pickles **crostini**

42

simple smoked salmon **snack**

46

seafood **bruschetta**

50

seafood bruschetta

Be sure to spoon the seafood sauce over the bruschetta just before serving. To prepare ahead of time, proceed as far as the thickened sauce and set aside. After an hour or two, reheat the sauce, add the seafood, and finish cooking.

Serves 4

30 minutes

1 hour

20–25 minutes

2

8	ounces (250 g) mussels, in shell	1	red bell pepper (capsicum), seeded and diced
8	ounces (250 g) clams, in shell	1	teaspoon saffron, dissolved in 1/2 cup (125 ml) warm milk
2	tablespoons extra-virgin olive oil		Salt and freshly ground black pepper
3	cloves garlic, 2 whole and 1 finely chopped	8	ounces (250 g) small squid, precooked
2	tablespoons coarsely chopped fresh parsley	8	ounces (250 g) shrimp (prawns), heads removed, shelled, and chopped
1	cup (250 ml) dry white wine	8	large slices firm-textured (homestyle) bread
1/2	tablespoon butter		
1	scallion (spring onion), finely chopped		

1. Soak the mussels and clams in a large bowl of cold water for at least an hour to purge them of sand. Pull the beards off the mussels and scrub well. Rinse thoroughly under cold running water.

2. Preheat the oven to 350°F (180°C/gas 4).

3. Heat 1 tablespoon of oil, 1 whole clove of garlic, and 1 tablespoon of parsley in a large frying pan over medium heat. Add the mussels and clams and pour in half the wine. Cover the pan and place over medium-high heat until all the shellfish are open. Drain the liquid they have produced into a bowl, strain, and set aside. Discard any shells that have not opened. Detach the mussels and clams from their shells and set aside.

4. Heat the remaining 1 tablespoon of oil with the butter in a large frying pan over medium heat. Add the chopped garlic, scallion, and bell pepper and sauté until beginning to soften, 2–3 minutes.

5. Add the remaining 1/2 cup (125 ml) wine and simmer until evaporated. Add the mussel liquid and saffron mixture. Season with salt and pepper. Simmer until the sauce is thick, 5–10 minutes. Add the mussels, clams, shrimp, and squid and simmer until heated through, 2–3 minutes.

6. Meanwhile, spread the bread out on a baking sheet and bake in the oven for about 5 minutes, until crisp and pale golden brown.

7. Rub each slice of toast with some garlic and spoon the warm seafood sauce over the top. Sprinkle with the remaining 1 tablespoon of parsley and serve warm.

italian sausage crostini

Taleggio is a fairly soft Italian cheese made from cow's milk. Replace with coarsely grated Fontina or Cheddar cheese in this recipe if you can't find it.

Serves 6

10 minutes

10 minutes

1 baguette (French loaf), thinly sliced on the diagonal (18–20 slices)

4 fresh Italian pork sausages, about 12 ounces (350 g), casings removed

5 ounces (150 g) Taleggio cheese

1 tablespoon fennel seeds

1

1. **Preheat** the oven to 350°F (180°C/ gas 4)

2. **Spread** the bread out on a baking sheet and bake in the oven for about 5 minutes, until crisp and pale golden brown.

3. **Mix** the sausage, cheese, and fennel seeds in a small bowl. Spread the mixture over the lightly toasted bread.

4. **Bake** until bubbling and browned, about 5 minutes. Serve hot.

If you liked this recipe, you will love these ones too:

porcini mushroom **crostini**

38

tuscan chicken liver **crostini**

54

fried polenta pieces with mushroom sauce

58

tuscan chicken liver crostini

This is a traditional Tuscan appetizer or snack. It is served everywhere, from restaurants and trattoria, to cafés, bars, and private homes. It really is delicious and surprisingly easy to make.

Serves 6–8

30 minutes

25–30 minutes

2

3	tablespoons butter
1	onion, finely chopped
1	pound (500 g) chicken livers, finely diced
	Salt and freshly ground black pepper
½	cup (125 ml) dry white wine
½	cup (125 ml) beef stock
¼	cup (60 ml) extra-virgin olive oil

4	anchovy fillets, finely chopped
2	tablespoons brine-cured capers, drained and finely chopped
1	baguette (French loaf), sliced
	Fresh basil leaves, to garnish

1. **Preheat** the oven to 350°F (180°C/ gas 4)

2. **Melt** 2 tablespoons of butter in a small frying pan over medium heat. Add the onion and sauté until softened, 3–4 minutes.

3. **Add** the chicken livers and cook, stirring often, for 5 minutes. Season with the salt and pepper. Pour in the wine and cook, stirring often, for 15 minutes more. Gradually add the beef stock as the mixture dries out. Remove from the heat and set aside to cool.

4. **Place** the liver mixture on a chopping board and chop with a large knife.

5. **Spread** the bread out on a baking sheet and bake in the oven for about 5 minutes, until crisp and pale golden brown.

6. **Heat** the oil in a medium saucepan over medium heat. Add the liver mixture, anchovies, and capers. Stir in the remaining butter and simmer for 3 minutes more.

7. **Spread** the liver mixture evenly over the crostini. Serve warm.

If you liked this recipe, you will love these ones too:

tuscan bruschetta **fingers**

32

porcini mushroom **crostini**

38

italian **sausage** crostini

52

fried polenta with mushrooms, peas & cheese

Serves 4–6

15 minutes

25–30 minutes

2

2	tablespoons extra-virgin olive oil
8	ounces (250 g) white mushrooms, sliced
1	cup (150 g) fresh or frozen peas
1	tablespoon brine-cured capers, drained
	Salt and freshly ground black pepper
½	cup (75 g) all-purpose (plain) flour
6	large slices cold polenta, storebought or homemade (see page 58)
1	large egg, lightly beaten
1	cup (150 g) fine dry bread crumbs
2	cups (500 ml) vegetable oil, for frying
5	ounces (150 g) mozzarella cheese, sliced
	Fresh basil, to garnish

1. Preheat the oven to 400°F (200°C/ gas 6).

2. Heat the olive oil in a large frying pan over medium heat. Add the mushrooms and peas. Mix well and simmer until almost tender, about 5 minutes.

3. Add the capers and season with salt and pepper. Simmer over low heat until the vegetables are tender, 3–4 minutes.

4. Lightly flour the polenta slices, dip them in the egg, and then into a bowl containing the bread crumbs.

5. Heat the frying oil in a large deep-fryer or deep saucepan until very hot.

Test the oil temperature by dropping in a small piece of bread. If it immediately bubbles to the surface and begins to turn golden, the oil is ready.

6. Fry the polenta slices in batches until golden brown, about 5 minutes each batch. Scoop out with a slotted spoon and drain on paper towels.

7. Cover each slice of polenta with a spoonful of peas and mushrooms and a slice of mozzarella.

8. Bake for 5–10 minutes, until the cheese is melted and golden. Sprinkle with the basil and serve hot.

If you liked this recipe, you will love these ones too:

pear & hazelnut **crostini**

34

porcini mushroom **crostini**

38

fried polenta pieces with mushroom sauce

58

fried polenta pieces
with mushroom sauce

If porcini mushrooms are out of season or unavailable, use the same quantity of mixed wild mushrooms or white cultivated mushrooms. If short of time, buy readymade polenta.

Serves 8–12

30 minutes

12 hours

1 hour

2

POLENTA

2	quarts (2 liters) cold water
2	tablespoons coarse sea salt
3½	cups (500 g) polenta (coarse-grain yellow cornmeal)

MUSHROOM SAUCE

2	pounds (1 kg) porcini mushrooms
2	cloves garlic, minced
⅓	cup (90 ml) extra-virgin olive oil
2	tablespoons finely chopped fresh thyme + extra, to garnish
	Salt and freshly ground black pepper
2	cups (500 ml) vegetable oil, for frying

1. **To prepare the polenta,** bring the water and salt to a boil in a saucepan large enough to hold at least 4 quarts (4 liters) of liquid. Add the cornmeal gradually, stirring constantly so that no lumps form. Stir over medium heat by moving a long, wooden spoon in a circular motion until the polenta begins to draw away from the sides of the pot on which a thin crust will form. The polenta should be stirred almost constantly for the 40–45 minutes it takes to cook.

2. **Pour** the cooked polenta onto a serving board. Let cool and harden overnight before frying.

3. **To prepare the mushroom sauce,** detach the stalks from the caps of the mushrooms. Coarsely chop both the stalks and caps.

4. **Heat** the olive oil in a large frying pan over medium heat. Add the garlic and sauté until pale gold, 3–4 minutes. Add the mushroom stalks first (they need longer to cook than the caps) and after about 5 minutes, add the caps.

5. **Add** the thyme and season with salt and pepper. Simmer until tender. The time the porcini take to cook will depend on how fresh they are. Don't let them become mushy.

6. **Cut** the cooled polenta into slices about 1/2 inch (1 cm) thick.

7. **Heat** the frying oil in a large deep-fryer or deep saucepan until very hot. Test the oil temperature by dropping in a small piece of bread. If it immediately bubbles to the surface and begins to turn golden, the oil is ready.

8. **Fry** the polenta slices in batches until golden brown, about 5 minutes each batch. Scoop out with a slotted spoon and drain on paper towels.

9. **Spoon** the mushroom sauce onto the hot polenta slices. Garnish with the extra thyme and serve immediately.

brie & peach tartlets

If liked, replace the peaches in this recipe with fresh nectarines or plums.
If fresh fruit is out of season, use well-drained canned peaches.

Serves 8

15 minutes

12–15 minutes

1

1	sheet frozen puff pastry (about 8 ounces/250 g), thawed
6	ounces (200 g) brie cheese, outer crust removed, and cut into small cubes
2	medium ripe yellow peaches, peeled, diced, and cut into small cubes
3	large thin slices prosciutto, diced
1	tablespoon finely chopped fresh thyme

1. **Preheat** oven to 400°F (200°C/gas 6). Set out one 24-cup mini muffin tin and one 12-cup mini muffin tin.

2. **Roll** out the pastry on a lightly floured work surface into a 14 inch (35 cm) square. Cut into 36 equal squares.

3. **Place** a square of pastry in each mini muffin cup. Place equal amounts of cheese, peach, and prosciutto in each of the pastry-lined cups.

4. **Bake** for 12–15 minutes, until puffed and golden brown. Sprinkle with the thyme. Serve warm.

If you liked this recipe, you will love these ones too:

prosciutto, peach & blue cheese **crostini**

40

palmiers **with pine nuts & parmesan**

78

blue cheese bites

86

vol-au-vents
with cream sauce & shrimp

 Serves 8–10

🍴 25 minutes

🔥 20 minutes

🍸 1

36	small shrimp (prawn) tails, deveined
2	tablespoons butter
3	tablespoons all-purpose (plain) flour
1	cup (250 ml) milk
	Few drops freshly squeezed lemon juice

1	tablespoon finely chopped fresh chives
1	teaspoon sweet paprika
	Salt and freshly ground black pepper
24	readymade mini vol-au-vent cases

1. **Preheat** the oven to 400°F (200°C/gas 6). Oil a large baking dish and line with waxed paper.

2. **Bring** a medium pan of salted water to a boil over medium-high heat. Add the shrimp and cook for 1 minute. Drain and let cool. Peel and coarsely chop half the shrimp tails.

3. **Melt** the butter in a small pan over low heat. Add the flour and cook over low heat for 2 minutes, stirring constantly. Remove from the heat and pour in the milk all at once.

4. **Stir** constantly over low heat until thick and smooth, 3–5 minutes. Remove from the heat and stir in the chopped shrimp, lemon juice, chives, paprika, salt, and pepper.

5. **Fill** the cases with the shrimp mixture. Decorate some of the vol-au-vents with the whole shrimp tails. Arrange in the prepared dish.

6. **Bake** for about 10 minutes, until the pastry is golden brown. Serve hot or at room temperature.

If you liked this recipe, you will love these ones too:

taramasalata

30

tuna vol-au-vents

64

garlic shrimp

160

tuna vol-au-vents

Vol-au-vent is a French term that translates literally as "flying in the wind." The name refers to the fact that the puff pastry shells should be light enough to blow away in the wind.

Serves 4

15 minutes

10 minutes

1

8	readymade medium vol-au-vent pastry cases	
2	tablespoons butter	
2	scallions (spring onions), finely chopped	
2	tablespoons all-purpose (plain) flour	
1	cup (250 ml) milk + extra, if needed	
$1/3$	cup (50 g) freshly grated mild cheese	

Finely grated zest of 1 lemon

$1/4$ cup (60 ml) freshly squeezed lemon juice

1 cup (200 g) canned tuna, drained and flaked

Salt and freshly ground black pepper

1 tablespoon finely chopped fresh chives

1. Preheat the oven to 350°F (180°C/gas 4). Put the vol-au-vent cases on a baking sheet and bake for 8–10 minutes, until golden brown. Place on a wire rack to crispen and cool a little.

2. Heat the butter in a small saucepan over medium heat. Add the scallion and sauté until softened, 2–3 minutes.

3. Add the flour and cook for 1 minute. Gradually pour in the milk, stirring constantly until the mixture is thick and smooth, 3–5 minutes.

4. Add the cheese, lemon zest and juice, and tuna. Stir until heated through. Season with salt and pepper. Add a little more milk if mixture is too thick.

5. Spoon the tuna mixture evenly into the vol-au-vents cases and sprinkle with the chives. Serve warm.

If you liked this recipe, you will love these ones too:

smoked salmon **dip**

28

tuna & pickles **crostini**

42

vol-au-vents with cream sauce & shrimp

62

Bready
Things

pretzels

Pretzels are a crisp German bread traditionally made in a knot-shape and sprinkled with coarse salt. They make a delicious snack with beer or predinner drinks.

Serves 6–12

45 minutes

2 hours

15 minutes

2

½ ounce (15 g) fresh yeast or 1 (¼-ounce/7-g) package active dry yeast
½ teaspoon sugar
1 cup (250 ml) warm water

2 cups (300 g) all-purpose (plain) flour
¼ teaspoon salt
1 large egg, lightly beaten
2 tablespoons coarse salt

1. **Combine** the yeast and sugar in a small bowl with 1/3 cup (90 ml) of the water. Stir well and set aside until foamy, 5–10 minutes.

2. **Sift** the flour and salt into a large bowl. Use a wooden spoon to gradually stir in the yeast mixture. Add enough of the remaining water to make a soft dough.

3. **Transfer** the dough to a lightly floured work surface and knead until smooth and elastic, 5–10 minutes. Shape into a ball and place in an oiled bowl. Cover with a cloth and set aside in a warm place until doubled in bulk, about 2 hours.

4. **Preheat** the oven to 450°F (225°C/gas 8). Turn the dough out onto a floured work surface and divide into 12 portions.

5. **Roll out** each portion into a long rope and make into a pretzel shape by twisting the ends around each other. Bring both ends back to the center of the strip. Arrange the pretzels, well-spaced, on baking sheets.

6. **Brush** with the egg and sprinkle with the salt. Bake for about 15 minutes, until well-risen and golden brown.

7. **Serve warm** or at room temperature.

If you liked this recipe, you will love these ones too:

bread **rings**

70

oregano **breadsticks**

72

palmiers with pine nuts & parmesan

78

bread rings

These crisp little crackers come from the southern Italian region of Puglia, where they are known as *taralli* or *tarallucci*. This recipe makes a large quantity but they can be stored in an airtight container for several weeks. If liked, flavor the dough with fennel seeds, chiles, or cumin.

Serves 20

45 minutes

20 minutes

1 hour

3

6⅔	cups (1 kg) all-purpose (plain) flour
1	tablespoon salt
1½	cups (375 ml) dry white wine
1	cup (250 ml) extra-virgin olive oil

1. **Sift** the flour and salt into a large bowl. Stir in the wine and enough oil to make a firm dough.

2. **Knead** the dough on a lightly floured work surface until smooth and elastic, 15–20 minutes. Cover and let rest for 20 minutes.

3. **Preheat** the oven to 400°F (200°C/gas 6). Oil three large baking sheets.

4. **Break off** pieces of dough and shape into small batons, about $1/2$ inch (1 cm) in diameter and 3 inches (8 cm) in

length. Shape into rings, pinching the ends together with your fingertips.

5. **Bring** a large pot of salted water to a boil. Cook the bread rings in batches for 2–3 minutes. Remove with a slotted spoon and transfer to a clean cloth to dry.

6. **Arrange** the bread rings on the baking sheets. Bake for 30–40 minutes, or until crisp and golden brown.

7. **Let cool** on wire racks. Serve at room temperature.

If you liked this recipe, you will love these ones too:

pretzels

68

oregano **breadsticks**

72

parmesan puffs

74

oregano breadsticks

Breadsticks, or *grissini* as they are known in Italy, come from the northern Italian city of Turin. They were invented in 1679 by the Turinese baker Antonio Brunero for the young prince and future king, Amedeo di Savoia. Vary the flavoring by replacing the oregano with crumbled dried chiles, fried onions, or fennel seeds.

Serves 12

45 minutes

1³/₄ hours

15–20 minutes

2

1	recipe basic bread dough (see page 84)	
¹/₄	cup (60 g) lard (or butter), melted	
3	tablespoons extra-virgin olive oil	

3 tablespoons finely chopped fresh oregano or 2 teaspoons dried oregano

1. **Prepare** the bread dough following the instructions on page 84. Gradually work the lard and oregano into the dough as you knead. Let rise in a warm place for 1¹/₂ hours.

2. **Preheat** the oven to 400°F (200°C/gas 6). Oil two large baking sheets.

3. **Punch** the dough down and knead briefly on a floured work surface.

Break off pieces of dough about the size of an egg and roll into logs about 12 inches (30 cm) long. Place on the prepared baking sheets, spacing well. Brush with the oil and let rise for 15 minutes.

4. **Bake** for 15–20 minutes, until crisp and golden brown. Cool on wire racks. Serve at room temperature.

If you liked this recipe, you will love these ones too:

pretzels

68

bread rings

70

cheese-filled barquettes

82

parmesan puffs

Serve these light and elegant little cheese puffs with a glass of wine before dinner.

Serves 4–6

30 minutes

20–25 minutes

3

¾	cup (120 g) shelled almonds
⅔	cup (150 ml) cold water
4	tablespoons (60 g) butter
1	cup (150 g) all-purpose (plain) flour
	Salt

¾	cup (90 g) freshly grated Parmesan cheese
	Pinch of hot paprika
2	large eggs

1. Preheat the oven to 400°F (200°C/gas 6). Butter a baking sheet and dust with flour.

2. Blanch and peel the almonds by placing them in a bowl and pour boiling water over the top so they are barely covered. Leave for 1 minute. Drain and rinse under cold water. Pat dry and slip off the skins. Chop finely in a food processor.

3. Combine the cold water with 3 tablespoons of butter in a small saucepan. Place over medium heat. When the water starts to boil, remove the pan from the heat and incorporate the flour and salt, stirring constantly with a wooden spoon.

4. Return the saucepan to the heat and cook until the dough is thick, stirring all the time. Remove from the heat and stir in the Parmesan and paprika. Set aside to cool a little. Add the eggs to the dough one at a time, stirring vigorously.

5. Transfer to a pastry bag with a smooth opening about 1/4 inch (5 mm) in diameter. Pipe marble-size balls of dough onto the baking sheet, spacing well. Sprinkle with the almonds, making sure they stick to the puffs.

6. Bake for 15–20 minutes, until puffed and lightly golden. Serve warm or at room temperature.

If you liked this recipe, you will love these ones too:

herb **rolls**

120

easy potato **knishes**

242

fried parmesan puffs

278

garbanzo bean flatbread

This unusual bread comes from the Tuscan coast, where it is known as *cecina* or *farinata*. It is served piping hot as a snack or appetizer.

Serves 8–12

5 minutes

4–12 hours

25–30 minutes

3

4	cups (600 g) garbanzo bean (chickpea) flour
1	tablespoon salt
4	cups (1 liter) cold water
1/2	cup (120 ml) extra-virgin olive oil

Freshly ground black pepper

Fresh basil leaves, to garnish

1. **Combine** the garbanzo bean flour and salt in a large bowl. Make a well in the center and use a wooden spoon to gradually stir in enough of the water to form a thick pouring batter. Set aside to rest for at least 4 hours or overnight.

2. **Preheat** the oven to 400°F (200°C/gas 6). Set out a large nonstick roasting pan.

3. **Pour** the oil into the roasting pan. Pour the batter into the pan, filling to a depth of $1/4$ inch (5 mm).

4. **Bake** for 8–10 minutes, until a thin crust forms on the surface.

5. **Transfer** to a serving dish and season generously with pepper. Serve hot with a few basil leaves to garnish.

If you liked this recipe, you will love these ones too:

bread rings

70

oregano breadsticks

72

parmesan puffs

74

palmiers with pine nuts & parmesan

These savory palmiers are as simple and quick to prepare as they are delicious to eat.

Serves 4–6

15 minutes

45 minutes

10–15 minutes

1

1	(8-ounce/250-g) sheet frozen puff pastry, thawed
1	large egg yolk, beaten
1/4	cup (45 g) pine nuts
1/2	cup (60 g) freshly grated Parmesan cheese

1. **Preheat** the oven to 350°F (180°C/gas 4). Oil a large baking sheet.

2. **Unroll** the pastry on a lightly floured work surface. Brush with the egg yolk. Sprinkle with the pine nuts and Parmesan.

3. **Roll** up the pastry starting from one edge and rolling until you reach the center. Roll up the remaining pastry starting from the opposite edge to make a double roll.

4. **Chill** the pastry roll in the refrigerator for 45 minutes. Use a sharp knife to cut into slices 1/4 inch (5 mm) thick.

5. **Arrange** on the baking sheet. Bake for 10–15 minutes, until golden brown.

6. **Serve warm** or at room temperature.

If you liked this recipe, you will love these ones too:

parmesan puffs

74

puff pastry vegetable parcels

248

tomato & pesto puff

262

herb mayonnaise barquettes

If you don't have barquette molds of exactly this shape and size, use any small tartlet pans or molds. If they are larger, you may need to bake them for a little longer.

- Serves 6–8
- 30 minutes
- 30 minutes
- 12–15 minutes
- 2

2	cups (300 g) all-purpose (plain) flour
$1/4$	teaspoon salt
$2/3$	cup (150 g) butter
2–3	tablespoons cold water
2	hard-boiled eggs, chopped
2	tablespoons finely chopped fresh parsley
2	tablespoons finely chopped fresh marjoram
1	cup (250 ml) mayonnaise

1. Sift the flour and salt into a medium bowl. Use a pastry blender to cut in the butter until the mixture resembles coarse crumbs. Add enough water to form a smooth dough.

2. Press the dough into a disk, wrap in parchment paper, and refrigerate for 30 minutes.

3. Preheat the oven to 350°F (180°C/ gas 4). Lightly oil 15 two-inch (5-cm) long fluted barquette molds.

4. Flour a clean work surface and roll out the dough to a thickness of $1/8$ inch (3 mm). Line the molds with the dough and prick with a fork.

5. Cover with parchment paper and fill with pie weights or dried beans. Bake for 12–15 minutes. Remove the paper and weights or beans, invert the molds, and set aside to cool.

6. Combine the eggs in a bowl with the parsley, marjoram, and mayonnaise. Fill the shells with the herb mayonnaise. Serve at once before the shells become soggy.

If you liked this recipe, you will love these ones too:

vol-au-vents **with cream sauce & shrimp**

62

tuna **vol-au-vents**

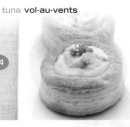

64

cheese-filled barquettes

82

cheese-filled barquettes

Barquette is French for "little boat" and these little savories are named for their shape. If preferred, you can line tartlet pans or muffins cups with the dough and fill them instead of shaping it by hand.

- 🍽 Serves 6–8
- ⏱ 30 minutes
- 🌡 1 1/2 hours
- 🍲 20–30 minutes

- 🍴 3

1	recipe basic bread dough (see page 84)
2	cups (500 ml) milk
3	tablespoons butter
3	tablespoons all-purpose (plain) flour
3	ounces (90 g) freshly grated Emmental cheese
8	ounces (250 g) freshly grated or sliced mozzarella cheese
4	ounces (120 g) freshly grated Fontina cheese Freshly ground black pepper

1. **Prepare** the bread dough following the instructions on page 84. Let rise in a warm place for 1 1/2 hours.

2. **Bring** the milk almost to a boil in a medium saucepan over medium heat.

3. **Melt** the butter in another medium saucepan. Add the flour and stir quickly for about 1 minute.

4. **Remove** the pan from the heat and add the hot milk all at once. Use a whisk to beat until smooth. Return to the heat and continue whisking until the sauce thickens.

5. **Add** the cheeses to the sauce and season with pepper. Stir until the cheeses are melted into the sauce. Remove from the heat.

6. **Preheat** the oven to 350°F (180°C/ gas 4).

7. **Break** the dough into 12 even-size pieces and roll each one out into a rectangle about 3 inches (8 cm) long. Roll up the edges a little to create a border then pinch the ends together to create a boat-shape. Spoon some filling into each barquette.

8. **Bake** for 10–15 minutes, until the bread is golden brown and the cheese filling is bubbling. Serve warm.

If you liked this recipe, you will love these ones too:

herb mayonnaise **barquettes**

80

blue cheese **bites**

86

tiropitas

88

spinach pies

These pies have a tangy spinach filling and make a refreshing snack or appetizer. Prepare in advance and pop into the oven to bake about 30 minutes before you are ready to serve.

Serves 6–8

40 minutes

2 hours

25–30 minutes

2

BASIC BREAD DOUGH

1	ounce (30 g) fresh compressed yeast or 2 ($\frac{1}{4}$-ounce/7-g) packages active dry yeast
1	teaspoon sugar
$1\frac{1}{2}$	cups (350 ml) water, warmed (110°F/ 43°C)
$3\frac{1}{4}$	cups (500 g) all-purpose (plain) flour
1	teaspoon salt
2	tablespoons extra-virgin olive oil

FILLING

2	small onions, finely chopped
1	teaspoon salt
1	pound (500 g) spinach, finely chopped
	Freshly ground black pepper
3	tablespoons freshly squeezed lemon juice
$\frac{1}{3}$	cup (90 ml) extra-virgin olive oil

1. **To prepare the bread dough,** combine the yeast and sugar in a small bowl. Add half the warm water and stir with until the yeast has dissolved. Set aside until frothy, 10–15 minutes.

2. **Sift** the flour and salt into a large bowl. Pour in the yeast mixture, most of the remaining water, and the oil. Stir until the flour is absorbed, adding more water as required.

3. **Transfer** the dough to a lightly floured work surface and shape into a ball. Press down on the dough with your knuckles to spread it. Take the far end of the dough, fold it a short distance toward you, then push it away again with the heel of your palm. Flexing your wrist, fold it toward you again, give it a quarter turn, then push it away. Repeat, gently and with the lightest possible touch, until the dough is smooth and elastic, shows definite air bubbles beneath the surface, and springs back if you flatten it with your palm, about 10 minutes.

4. **Transfer** to a large oiled bowl and cover with a cloth. Set aside until doubled in bulk, about $1\frac{1}{2}$ hours. To test, poke your finger into the dough; if the impression remains, it is ready.

5. **Preheat** the oven to 350°F (180°C/ gas 4). Oil two baking sheets.

6. **To prepare the filling,** sprinkle the onions with the salt. Mix in the spinach. Work the mixture in your hands until wilted and watery. Squeeze out excess moisture and place in a bowl. Stir in the pepper, lemon juice, and oil.

7. **Divide** the dough into walnut-size pieces. Roll into balls. Let rest for 15 minutes, then roll into flat disks.

8. **Spoon** a heaped teaspoon of filling onto the center of each disk. Fold the bottom left and right pieces into the middle and seal by pinching, then bring down the top piece to form a triangle and seal. Brush the tops with oil.

9. **Bake** for 25–30 minutes, until golden brown. Serve warm.

blue cheese bites

Use any tasty blue cheese, such as spicy Gorgonzola, Danish blue, or Roquefort.

Serves 6

15 minutes

2 hours

12–15 minutes

1

8	ounces (250 g) blue cheese	
5	ounces (150 g) cream cheese, softened	
	Freshly ground black pepper	
12	ounces (350 g) frozen puff pastry, thawed	
1	large egg, lightly beaten	

1. Preheat the oven to 400°F (200°C/ gas 6). Crumble the blue cheese into a bowl, combine with the cream cheese, and season with pepper.

2. Roll the pastry out into a thin sheet. Cut out 3 inch (8 cm) disks, rerolling the offcuts until all the pastry is used.

3. Place half the disks on a baking sheet. Moisten the pastry edges with some of the egg.

4. Divide the cheese mixture among the disks and cover with the remaining pastry disks. Ensure that the edges are sealed by pinching them together with your fingertips.

5. Make a small slit in the top of each savory to allow steam to escape. Brush with egg.

6. Bake for 12–15 minutes, until the pastry is golden brown. Serve warm.

If you liked this recipe, you will love these ones too:

prosciutto, peach & blue cheese **crostini**

40

gorgonzola & onion pizza **with fresh sage**

110

quick gorgonzola focaccia

124

tiropitas

These little Greek cheese pastries can also be made with store-bought phyllo pastry. Their name is a literal translation from the Greek for "cheese pies."

Serves 4

30 minutes

25–30 minutes

2

FILLING

8	ounces (250 g) crumbled feta cheese
1/4	cup (30 g) freshly grated Kefalotiri or Parmesan cheese
2	large eggs, lightly beaten
1	tablespoon finely chopped fresh dill
1	tablespoon finely chopped fresh mint
	Salt

YOGURT PASTRY

1 2/3	cups (250 g) all-purpose (plain) flour
1/2	cup (125 ml) plain yogurt
1/2	teaspoon salt
1	large egg, lightly beaten

1. Preheat the oven to 350°F (180°C/ gas 4). Set out a large baking sheet.

2. To prepare the filling, mix the feta, Kefalotiri, eggs, dill, and mint in a large bowl. Season with salt.

3. To prepare the yogurt pastry, mix the flour, yogurt, and salt in a large bowl to form a smooth dough.

4. Roll out the dough on a lightly floured work surface to about 1/8 inch (3 mm)

thick. Cut into 3 inch (8 cm) disks, rerolling the offcuts until all the pastry is used. You should get about 8 disks.

5. Use a teaspoon to divide the filling and place at the center of each disk. Fold the pastry in half over the filling and use a fork to seal the edges.

6. Arrange the tiropitas on the baking sheet and brush with the beaten egg. Bake for 25–30 minutes, until golden brown. Serve warm.

If you liked this recipe, you will love these ones too:

cheese-filled barquettes
82

filled focaccia **with goat cheese**
90

baby focaccias with cream cheese & prosciutto
96

filled focaccia
with goat cheese

The dough in these little filled focaccias does not contain salt. There is plenty of salt in the cheese filling which contrasts beautifully with the plain dough.

◉ Serves 4

🍲 30 minutes

🌡 1 hour

⏱ 10–15 minutes

🍸 2

1²⁄₃ cups (250 g) all-purpose (plain) flour
¹⁄₃ cup (90 ml) extra-virgin olive oil
8 tablespoons (120 ml) water
5 ounces (150 g) soft creamy goat cheese, such as chèvre or caprino

2 tablespoons finely chopped fresh thyme
Salt and freshly ground black pepper
1 large egg white
2 tablespoons water

1. Sift the flour into a large bowl. Add half the oil and 6 tablespoons of water. Mix to make a smooth dough. Shape into a ball and wrap in plastic wrap (cling film). Chill in the refrigerator for 1 hour.

2. Stir the goat cheese in a small bowl until smooth. Add the thyme and season with salt and pepper.

3. Preheat the oven to 400°F (200°C/ gas 6). Oil a large baking sheet.

4. Divide the dough into 8 pieces. Roll out on a lightly floured work surface into ¹⁄₄-inch (3-mm) thick disks.

5. Spread half the disks with the cheese mixture, leaving a ³⁄₄-inch (2-cm) border around the edges.

6. Beat the egg white and remaining 2 tablespoons of water in a small bowl. Brush the edges of the pastry with this mixture. Cover the filled focaccias with the remaining dough. Pinch the edges together to seal. Place on the prepared baking sheet. Brush with oil.

7. Bake for 5 minutes. Brush with the remaining oil. Bake for 5–10 minutes more, until puffed and golden brown. Serve hot.

If you liked this recipe, you will love these ones too:

tiropitas

88

ricotta & zucchini tartlets

100

filled pizzas with tomato & parmesan

106

baby focaccias
with tomato & prosciutto

Prosciutto is a salted, air-cured raw ham from Italy. Replace with other types of raw ham or use bacon in this recipe.

- Serves 6
- 35 minutes
- 1 1/2 hours
- 20–30 minutes
- 1

1	recipe basic bread dough (see page 84)
3	tablespoons extra-virgin olive oil
4	ounces (125 g) sliced prosciutto, cut into ribbons
1	small onion, thinly sliced
1	tablespoon salt-cured capers, rinsed and chopped
3	medium tomatoes, peeled and chopped
2	tablespoons finely chopped fresh parsley
2	tablespoons finely chopped fresh basil + extra leaves, to garnish

1. **Prepare** the basic bread dough following the instructions on page 84. Divide the dough into walnut-size balls and place, well-spaced, on a lightly floured work surface. Cover with a cloth and let rise until doubled in size, about 1 1/2 hours.

2. **Preheat** the oven to 375°F (190°C/ gas 5). Oil two baking sheets.

3. **Roll out** each ball of dough into a disk about 4 inches (10 cm) in diameter. Arrange the disks on the prepared baking sheets. Bake until golden brown, 12–15 minutes.

4. **While** the focaccias are in the oven, heat 2 tablespoons of oil in a small frying pan over medium heat. Add the prosciutto, onion, and capers and sauté until the onion is tender, about 5 minutes.

5. **Add** the tomatoes, parsley, and basil. Simmer until the tomatoes begin to break down, about 5 minutes. Stir in the remaining 1 tablespoon of oil.

6. **Place** the hot focaccias on serving dishes and spread each one with a little of the sauce. Serve hot, garnished with the extra parsley.

If you liked this recipe, you will love these ones too:

baby focaccias **with olives & pine nuts**
94

baby focaccias **with cream cheese & prosciutto**
96

filled pizzas **with tomato & parmesan**
106

baby focaccias
with olives & pine nuts

Bring a taste of the Mediterranean into your kitchen with this tasty recipe. Pine nuts are packed with flavor and protein but if you don't have them on hand replace with slivered almonds.

Serves 4–6

35 minutes

About 2 hours

35–45 minutes

1

1	recipe basic bread dough (see page 84)
1	small green bell pepper (capsicum)
1	small yellow bell pepper (capsicum)
1	small red bell pepper (capsicum)
3	tablespoons black olive paste

16	black olives, pitted and coarsely chopped
2	tablespoons pine nuts
	Salt and freshly ground black pepper
2	tablespoons extra-virgin olive oil

1. **Prepare** the basic bread dough following the instructions on page 84 and set aside to rise.

2. **Preheat** the oven to 425°F (220°C/gas 7). Oil two baking sheets.

3. **Bake** the bell peppers in the oven until dark and charred all over, 20–30 minutes. Place the hot bell peppers in a plastic bag. Close the bag and let rest for 10 minutes. Peel and seed the bell peppers. Slice thinly.

4. **Turn** the risen dough out onto a lightly floured work surface and knead for 5 minutes, adding the olive paste as you work.

5. **Divide** the dough into 16 equal portions and press into disks about $1/2$ inch (1 cm) thick. Place on the prepared baking sheets.

6. **Top** each disk with some of the peppers, olives, and pine nuts. Season with salt and pepper. Drizzle with the oil.

7. **Bake** for 15 minutes, until golden brown. Serve hot or at room temperature.

If you liked this recipe, you will love these ones too:

baby focaccias **with tomato & prosciutto**
92

onion, cheese & olive **triangles**
98

lebanese pizzas
108

baby focaccias with cream cheese & prosciutto

The milk in this pizza dough makes a softer, crumblier base than normal bread dough.

Serves 4–6

30 minutes

2 1/2 hours

30 minutes

2

DOUGH

1 ounce (30 g) fresh yeast or 2 (1/4-ounce/7-g) packages active dry yeast
1 tablespoon sugar
2/3 cup (150 ml) lukewarm milk
1 cup (150 g) whole-wheat (wholemeal) flour
1 cup (150 g) all-purpose (plain) flour
1/3 cup (50 g) cornstarch (cornflour)
Salt

TOPPINGS

5 ounces (150 g) Gorgonzola cheese
1/3 cup (90 ml) heavy (double) cream
3/4 cup (90 g) walnuts, coarsely chopped
5 ounces (150 g) cream cheese
1 tablespoon finely chopped fresh chives
2 teaspoons brine-cured green peppercorns, drained
1/3 cup (60 g) pine nuts
5 ounces (150 g) sliced prosciutto, cut in small squares

1. To prepare the baby focaccias, mix the yeast, sugar, and milk in a small bowl. Let stand until frothy, 10–15 minutes.

2. Sift both flours, the cornstarch, and salt into a large bowl. Stir the yeast mixture into the flour mixture to make a firm dough. Knead the dough on a lightly floured work surface until smooth and elastic, about 10 minutes. Place in an oiled bowl and set aside in a warm place until doubled in bulk, about 2 hours.

3. Preheat the oven to 400°F (200°C/gas 6). Cover two baking sheets with parchment paper.

4. Turn the dough out onto a lightly floured work surface and knead for 1–2 minutes.

5. Roll out the dough on a lightly floured work surface until 1/4 inch (5 mm) thick. Cut into 2-inch (5-cm) disks using a cookie cutter. Reroll the offcuts until all the dough is used.

6. Arrange the disks of dough on the prepared baking sheets. Bake until golden brown, about 15 minutes. Let cool on a wire rack.

7. To prepare the toppings, beat the Gorgonzola, cream, and walnuts in a bowl until well mixed. Beat the cream cheese, chives, green peppercorns, and pine nuts in another bowl.

8. Spread half of the disks with the Gorgonzola mixture and top half of them with a slice of prosciutto. Spread the other half of the disks with the cream cheese mixture and top half of them with a slice of prosciutto. Serve.

onion, cheese & olive
triangles

If you don't like olives, just leave them out. The onions, cheese, and herbs are delicious by themselves.

- Serves 6
- 30 minutes
- 1 1/2 hours
- 15–25 minutes
- 2

1	recipe basic bread dough (see page 84)
4	medium red onions, thinly sliced
3/4	cup (180 ml) water
4	tablespoons (60 ml) extra-virgin olive oil
1	tablespoon finely chopped fresh thyme
1	tablespoon finely chopped fresh rosemary
	Salt and freshly ground black pepper
1 1/4	cups (300 g) coarsely grated or thinly sliced mozzarella cheese
12	pitted black olives

1. **Prepare** the basic bread dough following the instructions on page 84 and set aside to rise.

2. **Cook** the onions with the water, 2 tablespoons of oil, and the thyme and rosemary in a large frying pan over medium heat until all the liquid has evaporated, 5–10 minutes. Season with salt, remove from the heat, and let cool.

3. **Preheat** the oven to 425°F (220°C/gas 7. Oil two large baking sheets.

4. **Turn** the risen dough out onto a lightly floured work surface and knead for 1–2 minutes. Roll out to about 1/8 inch (3 mm) thick and cut into triangles.

5. **Spread** some cheese, olives, and onion mixture on each triangle. Season with pepper and drizzle with the remaining 2 tablespoons of oil.

6. **Transfer** the triangles to the prepared baking sheets. Bake for 10–12 minutes, until the dough is golden. Serve hot or at room temperature.

If you liked this recipe, you will love these ones too:

filled focaccia **with goat cheese**

90

baby focaccias **with cream cheese & prosciutto**

96

pizzettas **with caramelized onions & blue cheese**

102

ricotta & zucchini tartlets

If making these tartlets during the summer months, buy zucchinis with the flowers attached and use them to make a spectacular garnish.

- Serves 8
- 30 minutes
- 1 3/4 hours
- 25–30 minutes

- 2

1 pound (500 g) basic bread dough (see page 84)
2 tablespoons extra-virgin olive oil
4 tender young zucchini (courgettes), thinly sliced
1 scallion (spring onion), thinly sliced
  Salt and freshly ground black pepper

1 1/4 cups (300 g) fresh ricotta cheese, drained
2 large eggs
1 tablespoon finely chopped fresh thyme
1/2 cup (50 g) chopped pistachios

1. **Prepare** the basic bread dough following the instructions on page 84 and set aside to rise.

2. **Heat** the oil in a large frying pan over medium heat. Add the zucchini and scallion and sauté until tender, about 5 minutes. Season with salt and pepper. Remove from the heat and let cool a little.

3. **Preheat** the oven to 400°F (200°C/gas 6). Set out eight 4-inch (10-cm) tartlet pans.

4. **Beat** the ricotta, eggs, and thyme in a large bowl.

5. **Roll** the dough out thinly on a lightly floured work surface. Divide into eight equal parts and line the tartlet pans. Let rise for 15 minutes.

6. **Reserve** a little of the zucchini mixture to garnish. Mix the rest into the ricotta mixture. Spoon evenly into the pans.

7. **Bake** for 10 minutes. Lower the oven temperature to 350°F (180°C/gas 4) and bake for 10–15 more minutes, until golden brown.

8. **Garnish** with the reserved zucchini mixture and pistachios and serve warm.

If you liked this recipe, you will love these ones too:

herb mayonnaise **barquettes**

80

baby focaccias **with cream cheese & prosciutto**

96

zucchini flower & rice tartlets

250

pizzettas with caramelized onions & blue cheese

These scrumptious little pizzas make a hearty snack.

Serves 6–8

45 minutes

2 hours

45 minutes

3

1	recipe basic bread dough (see page 84)	4	ounces (125 g) blue cheese, crumbled
1	cup (250 ml) extra-virgin olive oil, for frying	1	teaspoon finely chopped fresh oregano + extra, to garnish
2	red onions, thinly sliced		

1. **Prepare** the basic bread dough following the instructions on page 84 and set aside to rise.

2. **Heat** 1 tablespoon of oil in a medium frying pan over low heat. Add the onions and sweat until they caramelize, about 30 minutes.

3. **Remove** the onion mixture from the heat and stir in 2 ounces (60 g) of the blue cheese and the oregano.

4. **Divide** the risen dough into 12 even-size pieces and shape into balls. Cover with a cloth and let rise for 30 minutes.

5. **Roll** the dough balls out on a lightly floured surface into $1/4$-inch (5-mm) thick rounds. The edges should be slightly higher than the center.

6. **Heat** the oil in a large frying pan to very hot. Fry the pizzas in small batches until golden, spooning the oil over them. This will help them swell up. Drain well on paper towels.

7. **While the pizzettas are still warm,** top with the onion mixture and remaining cheese. Garnish with the extra oregano and serve hot.

If you liked this recipe, you will love these ones too:

onion, cheese & olive triangles

98

filled pizzas with tomato & parmesan

106

gorgonzola & onion pizza with fresh sage

110

pizzettas with ricotta & zucchini

Zucchini flowers (courgette blossoms) can be found in farmers markets and good fruit and vegetable stores during the summer months. Rinse them carefully before use.

Serves 8–10

20 minutes

2 hours

25 minutes

2

1	recipe basic bread dough (see page 84)
2	tablespoons extra-virgin olive oil
1	large shallot, finely chopped
3	tender young zucchini (courgettes), finely chopped
	Salt and freshly ground black pepper
1 ¼	cups (300 g) fresh ricotta cheese, drained
2	large eggs
1	tablespoon finely chopped fresh thyme
½	cup (50 g) chopped pistachios
10	cherry tomatoes, thinly sliced
6	large zucchini flowers (courgette blossoms), halved lengthwise (optional)

1. Prepare the basic bread dough following the instructions on page 84 and set aside to rise.

2. Preheat the oven to 400°F (200°C/ gas 6). Oil a large baking sheet.

3. Heat the oil in a large frying pan over medium heat. Sauté the shallot and zucchini until softened, about 5 minutes. Season with salt and pepper.

4. Beat the ricotta, eggs, and thyme in a large bowl.

5. Divide the dough into ten equal parts and shape into 3 inch (7.5 cm) disks.

Place on the prepared baking sheet. Let rise for 30 minutes.

6. Mix the zucchini mixture and pistachios into the ricotta mixture. Cover each of the pizzattas with a few slices of tomato. Spoon the ricotta mixture evenly over the top.

7. Bake for 10 minutes. Lower the temperature to 350°F (180°C/gas 4) and bake until golden, about 10 minutes more.

8. Garnish with the zucchini flowers, if you have them, and serve hot.

If you liked this recipe, you will love these ones too:

ricotta & zucchini **tartlets**

100

zucchini flower & rice tartlets

250

filled pizzas with tomato & parmesan

These wicked little filled pizzas come from Naples, the hometown of pizza. Be sure to serve them as soon as possible after frying.

Serves 4–6

20 minutes

2 hours

20 minutes

3

1	recipe basic bread dough (see page 84)
2	cups (500 ml) olive oil, for frying
1	(14-ounce/400-g) can storebought tomato sauce (for pasta or pizza)
1	cup (125 g) freshly grated Parmesan cheese
2	tablespoons finely chopped fresh basil
1	teaspoon dried oregano

1. **Prepare** the basic bread dough following the instructions on page 84 and set aside to rise.

2. **Divide** the risen dough into 12 even-size pieces and shape into balls. Cover with a cloth and let rise for 15 minutes.

3. **Roll** the dough balls out on a lightly floured work surface into 1/2-inch (5-mm) thick disks.

4. **Heat** the oil in a large frying pan to very hot. Fry the pizzas in small batches until golden, spooning the oil over them. This will help them swell up. Drain well on paper towels.

5. **Heat** the tomato sauce over low heat and stir in the Parmesan, basil, and oregano.

6. **Cut** a slice into the sides of the pizzas and spoon in the tomato sauce. Sprinkle with the extra Parmesan and serve hot.

If you liked this recipe, you will love these ones too:

baby focaccias **with tomato & prosciutto**
92

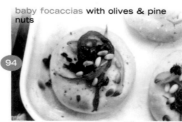
baby focaccias **with olives & pine nuts**
94

pizzettas **with caramelized onion & blue cheese**
102

lebanese pizzas

Serve these hearty pizzas straight from the oven. They are best piping hot.

- Serves 8–10
- 30 minutes
- 1¾ hours
- 55–65 minutes
- 2

1	recipe basic bread dough (see page 84)	1	teaspoon salt
4	tablespoons (60 ml) extra-virgin olive oil	1	teaspoon freshly ground black pepper
2	onions, finely chopped	1	teaspoon allspice
2	pounds (1 kg) coarsely chopped beef	½	teaspoon red pepper flakes
4	tablespoons pine nuts	1	teaspoon ground cinnamon
		1	cup (250 ml) plain yogurt

1. **Prepare** the basic bread dough following the instructions on page 84 and set aside to rise.

2. **Heat** the oil in a large frying pan over medium heat. Add the onions and sauté until softened, 3–4 minutes. Add the beef and sauté until browned, about 5 minutes.

3. **Add** the pine nuts, salt, pepper, allspice, red pepper flakes, and cinnamon. Simmer over low heat for 30 minutes. Remove from heat and stir in the yogurt.

4. **Preheat** the oven to 400°F (200°C/ gas 6). Oil two large baking sheets.

5. **Divide** the pizza dough into pieces about the size of an egg and roll into smooth balls. Cover and let rest for 15 minutes. Place the balls on the baking sheets and flatten to about ¼ inch (5 mm) thick. Spread with the topping.

6. **Bake** for 20–25 minutes, until the golden brown. Serve hot.

If you liked this recipe, you will love these ones too:

baby focaccias **with olives & pine nuts**
94

ricotta & zucchini **tartlets**
100

gorgonzola & onion pizza with fresh sage
110

gorgonzola & onion pizza
with fresh sage

Gorgonzola, sage, and onions make a delicious combo. Serve this pizza hot, straight from the oven.

- Serves 2–4
- 25 minutes
- 1 1/2 hours
- 20–30 minutes
- 1

1	recipe basic bread dough (see page 84)
1–2	tablespoons extra-virgin olive oil
	Salt
2–3	tablespoons finely chopped fresh sage
2	large white onions, peeled and thinly sliced into rings
5	ounces (150 g) Gorgonzola cheese, crumbled

1. **Prepare** the basic bread dough following the instructions on page 84 and set aside to rise.

2. **Preheat** the oven to 400°F (200°C/gas 6). Oil a 12-inch (30-cm) pizza pan.

3. **Transfer** the risen dough to a lightly floured work surface and knead for 1 minute. Use your fingertips to press it into the pan.

4. **Drizzle** with the oil. Sprinkle with the sage and then the onion rings. Season with salt.

5. **Bake** for 15–20 minutes, until the dough begins to brown. Sprinkle with the Gorgonzola and bake for 5–10 minutes more, until the cheese is bubbling and golden. Serve hot.

If you liked this recipe, you will love these ones too:

blue cheese **bites**

86

pizzettas with caramelized onion & blue cheese

102

quick gorgonzola **focaccia**

124

piquant onion pinwheels

If you don't like spicy food, leave the red pepper flakes out of the filling.

- Serves 6–8
- 45 minutes
- 2 hours
- 20 minutes

- 2

$\frac{1}{2}$	ounce (15 g) fresh yeast or 1 ($\frac{1}{4}$-ounce/7-g) package active dry yeast
1	tablespoon sugar
1	cup (250 ml) hot water
2	cups (300 g) all-purpose (plain) flour

1	teaspoon salt
5	tablespoons (75 g) butter
1	large egg, lightly beaten
4	large onions, thinly sliced
1	teaspoon red pepper flakes

1. **Combine** the yeast and sugar in a small bowl with $\frac{1}{2}$ cup (90 ml) of water. Stir well and let rest until frothy, 10–15 minutes.

2. **Sift** the flour and salt into a large bowl. Use a wooden spoon to gradually stir in the yeast mixture, 1 tablespoon of butter, and the egg. Add enough of the remaining water to make a soft dough.

3. **Transfer** to a lightly floured work surface and knead until smooth and elastic, 5–10 minutes.

4. **Cover** with a cloth and place in a warm place to rise until doubled in bulk, about $1\frac{1}{2}$ hours.

5. **Heat** the remaining 4 tablespoons (60 g) of butter in a large frying pan over medium heat. Add the onions and sauté until softened, 3–4 minutes. Season with the red pepper flakes.

6. **Turn** the dough out onto a floured work surface and roll into a rectangle about $\frac{1}{8}$ inch (3 mm) thick. Top with the onions. Roll the dough up tightly and slice thinly. Arrange, well-spaced, on a greased baking sheet and let rise for 30 minutes.

7. **Preheat** the oven to 350°F (180°C/gas 4).

8. **Bake** for 20–25 minutes, until golden brown. Serve warm or at room temperature.

If you liked this recipe, you will love these ones too:

onion, cheese & olive **triangles**

98

gorgonzola & onion pizza with fresh sage

110

cheese & tomato pinwheels

114

cheese & tomato pinwheels

Vary the cheese in these pinwheels according to what you like or have on hand. Cheddar, Fontina, Emmental, or Swiss Cheese will all work well.

- Serves 6–8
- 30 minutes
- 2 hours
- 20–25 minutes
- 2

½	ounce (15 g) fresh yeast or 1 (¼-ounce/ 7-g) package active dry yeast
1	teaspoon sugar
1	cup (250 ml) warm milk
2	cups (300 g) all-purpose (plain) flour
1	teaspoon salt
2	tablespoons butter, melted

4	ounces (125 g) finely chopped or grated mozzarella cheese
½	cup (125 ml) tomato paste (concentrate)
1	teaspoon dried oregano
½	cup (60 g) freshly grated Parmesan cheese

1. **Combine** the yeast and sugar in a small bowl with ⅓ cup (90 ml) of milk. Stir well and let rest until frothy, 10–15 minutes.

2. **Sift** the flour and salt into a large bowl. Add the butter, yeast mixture, mozzarella, and enough milk to make a soft dough.

3. **Transfer** to a lightly floured work surface and knead until smooth and elastic, 5–10 minutes. Shape into a ball and place in an oiled bowl. Cover with a clean cloth and let rise for 45 minutes.

4. **Turn** the dough out onto a lightly floured piece of parchment paper. Roll out into a rectangle about ⅛ inch (3 mm) thick.

5. **Spread** with the tomato paste. Sprinkle with oregano and Parmesan. Roll up the dough using the paper to help you. Wrap the roll of dough in the paper and chill in the refrigerator for 15 minutes.

6. **Unwrap** the dough and use a sharp knife to slice into ⅔-inch (1.5-cm) thick slices. Arrange on two oiled baking sheets and let rise for 1 hour.

7. **Preheat** the oven to 400°F (200°C/ gas 6).

8. **Bake** for 20–25 minutes, until golden brown. Serve hot or at room temperature.

If you liked this recipe, you will love these ones too:

baby focaccias with tomato & prosciutto
92

filled pizzas with tomato & parmesan
106

piquant onion pinwheels
112

zucchini & chive muffins

For a change, make these muffins with peeled and grated butternut squash instead of zucchini (courgettes).

- Serves 8
- 15 minutes
- 20–25 minutes

- 1

2 cups (300 g) all-purpose (plain) flour
2½ teaspoons baking powder
½ teaspoon salt
½ teaspoon coarsely ground black pepper
1 cup (125 g) freshly grated Gruyère, pecorino, or Parmesan cheese
2 large eggs

¾ cup (180 ml) milk or half-and-half (single cream) + more as needed
1 cup (150 g) finely grated zucchini (courgettes)
Bunch of fresh chives, snipped
1 tablespoon sunflower seeds, to sprinkle

1. **Line** a 12-cup muffin pan with paper liners. Preheat the oven to 400°F (200°C/gas 6).

2. **Combine** the flour, baking powder, salt, and pepper in a large bowl. Stir in the cheese.

3. **Whisk** the eggs and milk together in a medium bowl. Pour into the dry ingredients and mix with a fork until well combined, adding 1 or 2 extra tablespoons of milk, if needed. Stir in the zucchini and chives—the mixture will be lumpy.

4. **Spoon** the batter into the muffin cups. Sprinkle the tops with sunflower seeds.

5. **Bake** for 20–25 minutes, until risen, golden, and firm to the touch. Transfer to a rack and leave to cool. Serve at room temperature.

If you liked this recipe, you will love these ones too:

ricotta & zucchini **tartlets**

100

pizzettas **with ricotta & zucchini**

104

zucchini flower & rice tartlets

250

spicy corn bread

Corn is native to the Americas and local peoples have been making corn bread for centuries. There are many different types. Our recipe includes roasted chile peppers, another vegetable that originally came from America.

Serves 4

15–20 minutes

5 minutes

25–30 minutes

1

½ cup (75 g) all-purpose (plain) flour
1 teaspoon baking soda (bicarbonate of soda)
1 teaspoon baking powder
1 teaspoon salt
1 large egg
1 cup (250 ml) plain yogurt
⅔ cup (150 ml) half-and-half (single cream) or milk

1¾ cups (275 g) yellow cornmeal
3 tablespoons finely chopped bottled or canned roasted chile peppers
2 scallions (spring onions), finely chopped

1. Preheat the oven to 400°F (200°C/ gas 6). Lightly grease a square 8-inch (20-cm) cake pan with butter.

2. Sift the flour, baking soda, baking powder, and salt in a large bowl. Whisk the egg in a separate large bowl until frothy. Whisk in the yogurt and half-and-half.

3. Gradually stir the egg mixture into the flour mixture. Fold in the cornmeal in

batches until well blended. Mix in the chiles and scallions. Pour into the pan.

4. Bake for 25–30 minutes, until a skewer inserted into the center of the bread comes out clean.

5. Cool in the pan for 5 minutes. Cut into squares and serve warm.

If you liked this recipe, you will love these ones too:

zucchini & chive **muffins**

116

quick butternut & parmesan **loaf**

126

quick cheese & onion bread

130

herb rolls

Serve these rolls warm spread with butter or fresh cheese. Alternatively, fill them with sliced cheese, tomatoes, and chicken and add to school lunchboxes or a picnic hamper.

- 24 rolls
- 20 minutes
- 1 1/2 hours
- 20 minutes

- 2

1 1/2	ounces (45 g) compressed yeast or 3 ($^1/_4$-ounce/7-g) packages active dry yeast
1	tablespoon sugar
1 1/2	pounds (750 g) all-purpose (plain) flour
1	tablespoon salt
2	cups (500 ml) warm water
2	tablespoons dried herbs

(mixed tarragon, chervil, sage, marjoram, thyme, parsley, and basil)

1	teaspoon dried lavender flowers
4	tablespoons (60 ml) extra-virgin olive oil
1/2	cup (125 ml) sweet muscat dessert wine

1. **Combine** the yeast and sugar in a small bowl with $^1/3$ cup (90 ml) of water. Stir well and let rest until frothy, 10–15 minutes.

2. **Sift** the flour and salt into a large bowl. Add the yeast mixture, herbs, lavender flowers, oil, wine, and enough of remaining water to make a soft dough.

3. **Transfer** to a lightly floured work surface and knead until smooth and elastic, 5–10 minutes. Shape into a ball and place in an oiled bowl. Cover with a clean cloth and let rise until doubled in bulk, about 1 hour.

4. **Preheat** the oven to 400°F (200°C/ gas 6). Lightly oil two large baking sheets.

5. **Transfer** the risen dough to a lightly floured work and divide into 24 portions. Roll each piece into a ball and place about 2 inches (5 cm) apart on oiled baking sheets.

6. **Cover** with a cloth and leave to rise for 15 minutes. Make threes slashes in the top of each roll with a sharp knife.

7. **Bake** for 15–20 minutes, until golden risen and golden brown. Serve warm or at room temperature.

If you liked this recipe, you will love these ones too:

cheese & tomato **pinwheels**

114

whole-wheat **focaccia** with rosemary

122

apricot **bread**

134

whole-wheat focaccia
with rosemary

You can make this same focaccia with all-purpose (plain) white flour.

- Serves 4
- 25 minutes
- 2 hours
- 25–30 minutes

- 1

½ ounce (15 g) fresh yeast or 1 (¼-ounce/ 7-g) package active dry yeast

1 cup (250 ml) warm water

1⅔ cups (250 g) whole-wheat (wholemeal) flour

½ cup (75 g) all-purpose (plain) flour

Salt

1 tablespoon finely chopped rosemary + extra, to garnish

2 tablespoons extra-virgin olive oil

1. **Combine** the yeast with ⅓ cup (90 ml) of water in a small bowl. Stir well and let rest until frothy, 10–15 minutes.

2. **Sift** both flours and the salt into a medium bowl. Add the yest mixture and enough of the remaining water to obtain a soft dough.

3. **Turn out** onto a lightly floured work surface and knead until smooth and elastic, 5–10 minutes.

4. **Transfer** to an oiled bowl, cover, and let rise in a warm place until doubled in bulk, about 1½ hours.

5. **Turn out** onto a lightly floured work surface and knead, adding the rosemary as you work, 2–3 minutes.

6. **Oil** a 12-inch (30-cm) pizza or quiche pan. Press the dough into the pan using your fingers. Prick with a fork and drizzle with the oil. Let rise for 30 minutes.

7. **Preheat** the oven to 400°F (200°C/ gas 6).

8. **Bake** for 25–30 minutes, until golden brown. Serve hot or at room temperature garnished with a few leaves of fresh rosemary.

If you liked this recipe, you will love these ones too:

herb **rolls**

120

quick whole-wheat yogurt **bread**

128

apricot bread

134

quick gorgonzola focaccia

This delicious chewy focaccia is a must for Gorgonzola lovers. Serve warm with a green salad.

Serves 4–6

20 minutes

30–35 minutes

1

1¼ cups (300 ml) water
½ cup (125 g) butter, cut up
   Salt
2 cups (300 g) all-purpose (plain) flour
4 large eggs
8 ounces (250 g) Gorgonzola, cut into small cubes

1. **Put** the water in a large saucepan with the butter and a pinch of salt. Bring to a boil over medium heat. Remove from the heat and add the flour.

2. **Mix** until smooth then return to low heat. Simmer, stirring constantly, until the mixture comes away from the sides of the saucepan, 3–5 minutes. Remove from the heat and let cool slightly.

3. **Preheat** the oven to 350°F (180°C/gas 4). Oil a 10-inch (23-cm) springform pan.

4. **Beat** the eggs into the cooled dough mixture one at a time. Add 6 ounces (180 g) of Gorgonzola and mix well. Spoon the mixture into the prepared pan. Top with the remaining cheese.

5. **Bake** until risen and golden brown, 25–30 minutes. Serve warm.

If you liked this recipe, you will love these ones too:

cheese-filled **barquettes**

82

blue cheese **bites**

86

gorgonzola & onion pizza with fresh sage

110

quick butternut & parmesan loaf

This quick and healthy loaf is packed with vitamins, minerals, and protein. Serve warm.

Serves 6–8

15 minutes

10 minutes

45–50 minutes

1

- 1½ cups (225 g) all-purpose (plain) flour
- ½ teaspoon baking powder
- 1 tablespoon finely chopped fresh sage
- ½ cup (60 g) freshly grated Parmesan or pecorino cheese + extra for the top
- 1⅔ cups (250 g) grated butternut squash or pumpkin

- 12 black olives, pitted and chopped
- 2 large eggs
- 1 tablespoon milk
- 1 tablespoon pumpkin seeds, to sprinkle

1. **Preheat** the oven to 375°F (190°C/gas 5). Oil a baking sheet and set aside.

2. **Combine** the flour, baking powder, sage, Parmesan, butternut squash, and olives in a large bowl.

3. **Whisk** the eggs and milk in a separate bowl and stir into the flour mixture. Mix well and shape into a sticky ball.

4. **Flour** your hands, transfer the dough to the baking sheet, and pat into a round loaf. Sprinkle the top with pumpkin seeds and extra Parmesan.

5. **Bake** for 45–50 minutes, until the underside sounds hollow when tapped. Check after 30 minutes, and cover with aluminum foil if the top is browning too fast.

6. **Cool** on a rack for 10 minutes before slicing.

If you liked this recipe, you will love these ones too:

lebanese **pizzas**

108

zucchini & chive **muffins**

116

quick whole-wheat **yogurt** bread

128

quick whole-wheat
yogurt bread

Serve this bread warm or toasted spread with a little butter or low-fat fresh cheese.
It is also good with soups or salads.

Serves 6–8

15 minutes

55–60 minutes

1

3	cups (450 g) whole-wheat (wholemeal) flour + extra, to dust
1	tablespoon dark brown sugar
1	teaspoon salt
1/2	teaspoon sweet paprika
1	teaspoon baking soda (bicarbonate of soda)

2	cups (500 g) plain yogurt
1	teaspoon malt extract (optional)
1/3	cup (90 ml) milk
1/4	cup (45 g) pumpkin seeds
1	tablespoon sunflower seeds

1. **Preheat** the oven to 400°F (200°C/gas 6). Oil a 9 x 5-inch (23 x 12-cm) loaf pan.

2. **Combine** the flour, brown sugar, salt, paprika, and baking soda in a large bowl and mix well. Gradually add the yogurt and malt extract, if using. Stir in as much of the milk as needed to make a moist dough. For best results, mix everything together with your hands, although the dough is very sticky.

3. **Dust** your hands with a little flour and transfer the dough to the pan. Sprinkle the top with flour, and make a $2/3$-inch (1.5-cm)-deep cut lengthwise down the center with a knife. Sprinkle with the pumpkin and sunflower seeds.

4. **Bake** for 15 minutes. Decrease the heat to 350°F (180°C/gas 4) and bake for 40–45 minutes more, until brown and crisp on top.

5. **Cool** on a wire rack. Serve warm or toasted.

If you liked this recipe, you will love these ones too:

zucchini & chive **muffins**

116

herb **rolls**

120

whole-wheat **focaccia** with rosemary

122

quick cheese & onion bread

This delicious bread can also be served warm by itself or to accompany a bowl of soup or a fresh green salad. Spread with butter, if liked.

Serves 4–6

15 minutes

30 minutes

30–40 minutes

1

BREAD

1	cup (150 g) whole-wheat (wholemeal) flour
1	teaspoon baking powder
1	cup (125 g) freshly grated Parmesan cheese
4	scallions (spring onions), finely chopped
1	large potato, peeled and grated
1	large egg, lightly beaten
	Salt and freshly ground black pepper
2–3	tablespoons milk

TO SERVE

4–6	tablespoons light cream cheese or fresh creamy goat cheese, such as chèvre or caprino
4–6	cherry tomatoes, sliced
	Handful of baby arugula (rocket) leaves
	Freshly ground black pepper

1. Preheat the oven to 375°F (190°C/ gas 5). Oil a baking sheet.

2. Sift the flour and baking powder into a large bowl. Stir in the cheese, scallions, potato, and egg. Season with salt and pepper. Add 2 tablespoons of milk and stir the mixture with a wooden spoon to form a firm dough. Add the extra 1 tablespoon of milk if the mixture is too dry.

3. Shape the dough into a ball and place on the baking sheet. Bake for 40–45 minutes, until risen and golden brown. Let cool a little on a rack.

4. Slice thickly and spread with cheese. Top with the cherry tomatoes and arugula. Season with black pepper and serve.

If you liked this recipe, you will love these ones too:

spicy **corn bread**

118

quick butternut & parmesan **loaf**

126

quick savory **loaf**

132

quick savory loaf

Serve slices of this nourishing quick bread as an after-school or after-sports snack.

Serves 4–6

15 minutes

30–40 minutes

1

1 2/3 cups (250 g) all-purpose (plain) flour

1 teaspoon baking powder

4 large eggs

1/2 cup (125 ml) dry white wine

1/2 cup (125 ml) extra-virgin olive oil

8 ounces (250 g) ham, diced

5 ounces (150 g) salt pork or lardons (fat bacon), diced

1 1/2 cups (150 g) thinly sliced pitted black olives

1 1/4 cups (150 g) freshly grated Parmesan cheese

Salt and freshly ground black pepper

1. Preheat the oven to 350°F (180°C/gas 4). Butter a 5 x 9-inch (13 x 23-cm) loaf pan.

2. Sift the flour and baking powder into a large bowl. Make a well in the center and add the eggs, one at a time, stirring until just blended after each addition. Add the wine and oil and stir until smooth.

3. Stir in the ham, salt pork, olives, and cheese. Season with salt and pepper. Pour the batter into the prepared pan.

4. Bake for 30–40 minutes, until risen and a toothpick inserted into the center comes out clean.

5. Cool the loaf in the pan for 15 minutes. Turn out onto a rack. Serve warm or at room temperature.

If you liked this recipe, you will love these ones too:

quick gorgonzola **focaccia**

124

quick butternut & parmesan **loaf**

126

quick cheese & onion bread

130

apricot bread

Serve this bread with soft fresh cheeses, such as ricotta, cottage cheese, reduced-fat cream cheese, or robiola. When fresh apricots are out of season, use well-drained canned apricots.

- Serves 4–6
- 30 minutes
- 2 1/2 hours
- 30 minutes

- 2

1/2 ounce (15 g) fresh compressed yeast or 1 (1/4-ounce/7-g) package active dry yeast
1 teaspoon sugar
3/4 cup (180 ml) warm water +

extra, as required
2 cups (300 g) all-purpose (plain) flour
1/2 teaspoon salt
5 ripe apricots, halved
1 tablespoon vegetable oil

1. Mix the yeast, sugar, and water in a small bowl. Let stand until frothy, 10–15 minutes.

2. Oil a 9 x 5-inch (23 x 13-cm) loaf pan. Sift the flour and salt into a large bowl.

3. Stir the yeast mixture into the flour to make a firm dough. Add a little more warm water if the dough is too stiff. Knead the dough on a lightly floured work surface until smooth and elastic, 5–10 minutes.

4. Shape into a ball and place in an oiled bowl. Cover with a cloth and let rise in a warm place until doubled in bulk, about 2 hours.

5. Transfer the risen dough to the prepared pan and arrange the halved apricots on top. Cover and let rise in a warm place for 30 minutes.

6. Preheat the oven to 400°F (200°C/gas 6). Drizzle the oil over the top of the loaf.

7. Bake for about 30 minutes, until risen and golden brown. Serve warm or at room temperature.

If you liked this recipe, you will love these ones too:

cheese & tomato **pinwheels**

114

herb **rolls**

120

whole-wheat focaccia **with rosemary**

122

Fishy Fun

shrimp & papaya salad

Papayas are one of nature's wonderfoods. Rich in vitamin C, folate, and potassium, they contain a natural digestive aid called papain which cleans the digestive tract and aids digestion.

Serves 4

10 minutes

1

¼	cup (60 ml) Asian sesame oil
¼	cup (60 ml) freshly squeezed lime juice
1	large papaya (pawpaw), peeled, halved, and seeded

1¼	pounds (600 g) cooked shrimp (prawns), peeled and deveined
3	cups (150 g) curly endive leaves (frisée)

1. **Combine** the sesame oil and lime juice in a large bowl.

2. **Dice** the papaya into small cubes and add to the dressing. Add the shrimp and curly endive and toss well to combine.

3. **Divide** the salad evenly among four serving plates and serve.

If you liked this recipe, you will love these ones too:

crab & avocado **salad**

140

grilled octopus **salad**

142

seafood **salad**

144

crab & avocado salad

Serve this salad in tiny glasses for an elegant snack.

Serves 6–8

15 minutes

1

½ cup (125 g) mayonnaise
½ cup (125 g) sour cream
2 stalks celery, finely chopped
2 scallions (green onions), finely chopped
2 tablespoons fresh cilantro (coriander) + extra leaves, to garnish
1 teaspoon cayenne pepper
1 pound (500 g) cooked crab meat

¼ teaspoon Tabasco sauce
Salt and freshly ground black pepper
2 ripe avocados, peeled, pitted and cut into small cubes
1 small red bell pepper (capsicum), seeded and cut into small squares
Corn chips, to serve

1. Combine the mayonnaise, sour cream, celery, scallions, cilantro, cayenne pepper, crab meat, Tabasco, salt, and pepper in a medium bowl. Mix gently and well.

2. Divide the cubes of avocado evenly among 6–8 small serving glasses. Top with about half the bell pepper. Spoon the crab mixture in on top. Garnish the top of each serving with the remaining bell pepper and cilantro leaves.

3. Chill in the refrigerator until ready to serve. Serve with corn chips.

If you liked this recipe, you will love these ones too:

taramasalata

30

shrimp & papaya **salad**

138

crab cakes with roasted bell pepper sauce

166

grilled octopus salad

Be sure to cook the baby octopus quickly on a very hot grill plate. If it isn't cooked very rapidly it will become chewy and unappetizing.

Serves 6

20 minutes

12 hours

3–6 minutes

2

LIME & CHILE MARINADE

1/3	cup (90 ml) extra-virgin olive oil
	Freshly squeezed juice of 1 lime
1	fresh red chile, seeded and thinly sliced
1	clove garlic, finely chopped
1	pound (500 g) baby octopus, cleaned
	Salt and freshly ground black pepper

TOMATO CONCASSE

4	plum tomatoes, diced
3	tablespoons finely chopped fresh cilantro (coriander)
1/2	Spanish onion, diced
1/3	cup (90 ml) balsamic or sherry vinegar
1	tablespoon extra-virgin olive oil
1	tablespoon freshly squeezed lime juice
	Freshly ground black pepper

1. **To prepare the marinade,** combine the oil, lime juice, chile, and garlic in a medium bowl. Add the octopus, season with salt and pepper, and marinate in the refrigerator overnight.

2. **To prepare the tomato concasse,** combine the tomatoes, cilantro, onion, vinegar, oil, lime juice, and pepper in a small bowl.

3. **Preheat** a barbecue plate or char-grill pan to very hot.

4. **Drain** the octopus. Cook on the barbecue or in the pan, turning frequently, until tender, 3–6 minutes.

5. **Serve** the octopus hot with the tomato concasse spooned over the top.

If you liked this recipe, you will love these ones too:

seafood **salad**
144

pan-fried squid **with lemon**
174

deep-fried calamari with almond crust
176

seafood salad

This is a delicious and healthy snack to prepare ahead of time. Keep chilled in the refrigerator until just before serving. Serve with fresh bread or fingers of warm toast.

Serves 8

45 minutes

2–3 hours

30 minutes

3

1	pound (500 g) clams, in shell
1	pound (500 g) mussels, in shell
1	pound (500 g) octopus, cleaned
14	ounces (400 g) calamari, cleaned and sliced into rings
2	tablespoons salt
1	pound (500 g) raw shrimp (green prawns)
½	cup (125 ml) extra-virgin olive oil

Freshly squeezed juice of ½ lemon

2 cloves garlic, finely chopped

2 tablespoons finely chopped fresh parsley

Salt and freshly ground black pepper

½ teaspoon crushed dried chiles or red pepper flakes (optional)

1. **Soak** the clams and mussels in a large bowl of cold water for at least 1 hour. Pull the beards off the mussels. Scrub well and rinse in abundant cold water.

2. **Place** the octopus in a pot with 2½ quarts (2.5 liters) of cold water and 1 tablespoon of salt and bring to a boil over high heat. Lower the heat to a gentle simmer and cook until tender, about 1 hour.

3. **Add** the calamari rings and shrimp and simmer until the shrimp are pink, 2–4 minutes. Let the seafood cool in the cooking water for 15 minutes. Drain and set aside to cool.

4. **Shell** the shrimp and place in a salad bowl with the calamari. Chop the octopus into bite-size pieces and add to the salad bowl.

5. **Cook** the clams and mussels in a large frying pan over medium heat until they are all open. Discard any that do not open. Remove the mollusks from their shells and add to the salad bowl.

6. **Whisk** the oil, lemon juice, garlic, parsley, salt, pepper, and chiles, if using, in a bowl. Pour over the salad and toss well.

7. **Chill** in the refrigerator for at least 30 minutes before serving.

mexican ceviche

Ceviche with lime juice is a Mexican specialty. It is made by marinating the fish in the lime juice until it is "cooked" by the acids in the fruit. This is a very light and healthy snack.

Serves 6

30 minutes

3–12 hours

2

1 ¼	pounds (600 g) firm fish (such as sea bass, haddock, cod, monkfish, salmon, or tuna), skin and bones all carefully removed
	Freshly squeezed juice of 6–8 limes
1	large clove garlic, crushed
2	teaspoons finely grated ginger
1	tablespoon cider vinegar
¼	cup (60 ml) mild-flavored extra-virgin olive oil
¾	cup (180 ml) iced water
6	scallions (spring onions), white part only, thinly sliced
2	long red chiles, halved, seeded, and thinly sliced
4	plum tomatoes, peeled and chopped
2	bottled roasted red bell pepper (capsicum) halves, chopped
3	tablespoons coarsely chopped fresh cilantro (coriander) leaves
	Salt and freshly ground black pepper
6	tablespoons (90 ml) sour cream, to serve

1. **Thinly slice** the fish fillets into ½-inch (1-cm) cubes. Place in a medium bowl and pour in the lime juice. Toss gently, making sure the fish is completely coated in juice. Use more limes if needed. Marinate for at least 3 hours (or overnight) in the refrigerator.

2. **Blend** the garlic and ginger with the vinegar and oil in a liquidizer. Pour into a medium bowl.

3. **Stir** in the water. Add the scallions, chiles, tomatoes, bell peppers, and half the cilantro. Cover and marinate for at least 3 hours (or overnight) in the refrigerator.

4. **Just before** you are ready to serve, mix the marinated ingredients of both bowls together. Gently stir in the remaining cilantro and season with salt and pepper.

5. **Divide** among six serving bowls and top each one with 1 tablespoon of sour cream.

If you liked this recipe, you will love these ones too:

salmon carpaccio **with lemon & peppercorns**

142

oysters **on the half shell**

150

salmon carpaccio
with lemon & peppercorns

Choose the best fresh wild salmon you can buy for this dish. If you ask your fishmonger to clean and very thinly slice the salmon this snack can be prepared in just a few minutes.

Serves 8

15 minutes

4 hours

1

1	teaspoon coarse sea salt	
2	tablespoons brine-cured green peppercorns, drained	
1–2	teaspoons fresh thyme leaves	
½	cup (125 ml) extra-virgin olive oil	

Freshly squeezed juice of 1 lemon

1 pound (500 g) very fresh salmon fillet, thinly sliced

1 lemon, cut into wedges, to garnish

1. **Coarsely** pound the salt and half the peppercorns in a mortar and pestle. Add the thyme and mix well.

2. **Whisk** 1/3 cup (90 ml) of the oil with the lemon juice and salt mixture in a small bowl.

3. **Arrange** the salmon on a large serving dish and pour the dressing over the top. Cover with plastic wrap (cling film) and chill in the refrigerator for 4 hours.

4. **Remove** the plastic wrap and drizzle with the remaining oil. Garnish with the remaining peppercorns and the lemon wedges and serve.

If you liked this recipe, you will love these ones too:

smoked salmon **dip**
28

smoked salmon rolls **with goat cheese**
44

simple smoked salmon snack
46

oysters on the half shell

Fresh live oysters that taste of the open sea do not need anything except perhaps a squeeze of fresh lemon juice and a little hot sauce. Slurp them down with a glass of cold champagne.

Serves 4

10 minutes

2

24 very fresh oysters in shell
2 lemons, cut in wedges
Crushed ice, to serve
Tabasco sauce, to serve

1. **Rinse** the oysters well to remove any sand and grit from the shells. Wear gloves to protect your hands. Grip the oyster in one hand with a clean dish towel. Use an oyster knife or clean flat screw driver to carefully pry open the oysters. Loosen the oysters where they are attached to their shells so they will slip off easily.

2. **Set out** a large platter with a raised lip. Cover it with ice. Arrange the oysters on their half shells on top of the ice. Decorate with a few wedges of lemon. Serve the Tabasco on the side.

If you liked this recipe, you will love these ones too:

mussels & **clams**

152

stuffed **mussels**

154

baked **scallops** with mushrooms & béchamel

156

mussels & clams

The clams and mussels can be cleaned, soaked, and drained the night before. Store them in a large bowl in the refrigerator overnight. Rinse and drain in a colander the next day.

○ Serves 6–8

◑ 15 minutes

♨ 1 hour

⊙ 8–10 minutes

🍸 1

2 pounds (1 kg) clams, in shell
2 pounds (1 kg) mussels, in shell
2 tablespoons extra-virgin olive oil
2 tablespoons butter
Generous pinch of red pepper flakes
4 cloves garlic, minced
Freshly ground black pepper

2 tablespoons finely chopped fresh parsley
$\frac{1}{4}$ cup (60 ml) dry white wine
Freshly squeezed juice of 1 lemon
1 lemon, cut into wedges, for garnish
Fresh baguette (French loaf), to serve

1. **Soak** the clams and mussels in a large bowl of cold water for at least 1 hour. Pull the beards off the mussels. Scrub well and rinse in abundant cold water.

2. **Heat** the oil and butter in a large pot with a lid over medium-high heat. Add the red pepper flakes and garlic and sauté for 30 seconds. Add the clams and mussels and stir well. Crack some pepper into the pot, add the parsley, and then pour in the wine. Cover and simmer for 8–10 minutes.

3. **After 5 minutes,** check to see if most of the shells have opened and give them a stir. Cover and cook for a few minutes more. Discard any clams or mussels that have not opened after 10 minutes.

4. **Drizzle** the lemon juice over the shells. Ladle the shellfish into bowls with the cooking juices.

5. **Serve hot** with a wedge of lemon and slices of crusty bread to mop up the juices. Don't be afraid to use your fingers to scoop up some of the broth with the shells.

If you liked this recipe, you will love these ones too:

clam crostini

48

seafood salad

144

stuffed mussels

154

stuffed mussels

Low in calories and fat, mussels are an excellent source of protein and also a good source of omega-3 oils.

- Serves 2
- 20 minutes
- 1 hour
- 10–12 minutes

- 1

24	mussels, in shell	
1 ½	cups (100 g) fresh bread crumbs	
¼	cup (50 g) freshly grated Parmesan cheese	

1	cup (50 g) finely chopped fresh parsley
4	anchovy fillets, preserved in oil, ¼ cup (60 ml) of the oil reserved

1. Soak the mussels in a large bowl of cold water for at least 1 hour. Pull off any beards and scrub well. Rinse in abundant cold water.

2. Preheat the oven to 400°F (200°C/ gas 6).

3. Combine the bread crumbs, cheese, parsley, anchovies, and reserved anchovy oil in a medium bowl.

4. Open the mussels by inserting a short strong knife or oyster shucker near the hinge and twist to open the shell. Discard the top shells.

5. Place the mussels on a baking sheet. Top each one with bread crumb mixture.

6. Bake for 10–12 minutes. Serve hot.

If you liked this recipe, you will love these ones too:

mussels & clams
152

baked scallops with mushrooms & béchamel
156

baked scallops with prosciutto
158

baked scallops with mushrooms & béchamel

Scallops spoil very quickly and are almost always frozen immediately after harvest. However, you can usually buy them on the shells (already shucked, they have been replaced in the shells). If you have fresh unopened scallops, shuck with a small, strong shucking knife.

Serves 2–4

30 minutes

20–30 minutes

2

8	large fresh scallops, on the half shell (already detached)	mushrooms, coarsely chopped
4	tablespoons (60 g) butter	Salt and freshly ground black pepper
1	small onion, finely chopped	
1	clove garlic, finely chopped	2 tablespoons all-purpose (plain) flour
1/2	tablespoon finely chopped fresh thyme	1 1/2 cups (375 ml) milk
2	ounces (60 g) ham, chopped	4 tablespoons freshly grated Parmesan cheese
5	ounces (150 g) white	

1. Boil the scallop shells in a pot of water for a few minutes. Set aside to cool.

2. Preheat the oven to 400°F (200°C/gas 6).

3. Heat 2 tablespoons of butter in a medium saucepan over medium heat. Add the onion and garlic and sauté until softened, 3–4 minutes. Add the thyme, ham, and mushrooms. Season with salt and pepper and simmer until the mushrooms have released their moisture and are tender, 5–10 minutes.

4. Melt the remaining butter in a small saucepan over medium heat. Stir in the flour, mixing well. Remove from the heat and stir in the milk. Return to the heat, stirring constantly, and simmer until thickened, 3–5 minutes. Stir into the mushroom mixture.

5. Place the scallops back in the shells. Spoon some mushroom and béchamel mixture over each scallop. Sprinkle with the Parmesan.

6. Bake for 5–10 minutes, until the sauce is bubbling and golden brown. Serve hot.

If you liked this recipe, you will love these ones too:

mussels & clams

152

stuffed **mussels**

154

baked scallops with prosciutto

158

baked scallops with prosciutto

Scallops look so pretty when served in their shells. Fresh scallops in their shells are not always easy to find. If you do find them, keep the shells for future use.

Serves 4

10 minutes

5 minutes

1

1 pound (500 g) sea scallops
Salt and freshly ground black pepper

4 slices prosciutto, cut into squares about the size of the scallops

½ cup (75 g) fine dry bread crumbs

1 tablespoon finely chopped fresh parsley

1 teaspoon freshly squeezed lemon juice

¼ cup (60 ml) extra-virgin olive oil

1. Preheat the oven to 400°F (200°C/ gas 6).

2. Place two scallops in each scallop shell, if you have them, or divide them evenly among four ramekins or baking dishes. Season with salt and pepper. Cover the scallops in each shell or dish with a piece of prosciutto.

3. Combine the bread crumbs, parsley, lemon juice, and oil in a small bowl. Sprinkle over the scallops.

4. Place the shells or dishes on a baking sheet. Bake until just tender, about 5 minutes. Serve hot.

If you liked this recipe, you will love these ones too:

mussels & clams

152

stuffed mussels

154

baked scallops with mushrooms & béchamel

156

garlic shrimp

Shrimp are an excellent source of selenium and low-fat, low-calorie protein. Shrimp are also a very good source of vitamins B12 and D.

- Serves 6–8
- 10 minutes
- 30 minutes
- 6 minutes
- 1

2	pounds (1 kg) medium shrimp (prawn tails), peeled and deveined
4	cloves garlic, finely chopped
1	small fresh red chile, seeded and finely chopped
¼	cup (60 ml) extra-virgin olive oil

Freshly squeezed juice of 2 lemons
Freshly ground black pepper
Lime wedges, to garnish

1. Put the shrimp in a shallow dish. Whisk the garlic, chile, oil, lemon juice, and pepper in a small bowl. Pour this mixture over the shrimp and let marinate for 30 minutes.

2. Heat the marinade in a large frying pan over medium-high heat. Cook the shrimp in the marinade until pink and cooked through, about 3 minutes on each side (according to size).

3. Place the shrimp on individual serving dishes or on a large platter. Pour the juices from the pan over the top. Garnish with the lime and serve hot.

If you liked this recipe, you will love these ones too:

shrimp & papaya **salad**

138

seafood **salad**

144

shrimp skewers

172

grilled fish with spicy coconut chutney

This is a heart-healthy snack that you can also serve for lunch.

Serves 4

20 minutes

2 hours

3–5 minutes

2

FISH

2	tablespoons vegetable oil
2	tablespoons freshly squeezed lime juice
1	teaspoon garam masala
1/2	teaspoon ground turmeric
4	(8-ounce/250-g) skinless, firm white fish fillets, such as blue eye, snapper, rockfish, or grouper
	Salt and freshly ground black pepper
	Lime wedges, to serve

COCONUT CHUTNEY

1/4	fresh coconut, flesh removed and coarsely chopped
1	clove garlic, chopped
1	(1-inch/2.5–cm) piece ginger, peeled
1	green birds' eye chile, chopped
1/2	cup (25 g) chopped fresh mint
1/4	cup chopped fresh cilantro (coriander)
3	tablespoons freshly squeezed lime juice
1	cup (250 ml) plain yogurt
1/4	teaspoon salt
1	tablespoon vegetable oil
4	red birds' eye chiles
1	teaspoon black mustard seeds
1/4	teaspoon garam masala
1/4	teaspoon ground turmeric

1. **To prepare the fish,** combine the oil, lime juice, garam masala, and turmeric in a large bowl. Add the fish and toss to coat. Season with salt and pepper. Cover and refrigerate for at least 2 hours.

2. **To prepare the coconut chutney,** combine the coconut, garlic, ginger, green chile, mint, cilantro, and lime juice in a food processor and blend to make a coarse paste. Transfer to a medium bowl, add the yogurt and salt and stir to combine. Set aside.

3. **Heat** the oil in a small frying pan over medium heat. Add the whole red chiles and fry for 10–20 seconds. Add the mustard seeds, garam masala, and turmeric and cook for 30 seconds, until the seeds begin to pop and the spices are fragrant. Remove from the heat and set aside to cool.

4. **Add** the fried spices to the prepared coconut mixture and stir to combine. Transfer to a small serving dish. Cover and refrigerate until required.

5. **Heat** a barbecue plate or char-grill to medium-high heat. Lightly oil the hot plate and cook the prepared fish until tender, 2–3 minutes on each side.

6. **Serve** the fish hot with the coconut chutney and lime passed separately.

spinach & salmon pâté
with blackcurrant sauce

Fresh salmon and spinach are always a healthy combo. The sauce in this recipe is also packed with vitamins and goodness.

Serves 4

30 minutes

12 hours

1 hour

3

PÂTÉ

14	ounces (400 g) fresh salmon
3	large eggs
	Salt and freshly ground black pepper
	Pinch of freshly grated nutmeg
14	ounces (400 g) fresh spinach leaves, chopped
⅔	cup (150 ml) heavy (double) cream

SAUCE

⅓	cup (100 g) blackcurrant preserves (jam)
	Zest of ½ orange, in one long piece, removed with a sharp knife
	Freshly squeezed juice of 1 orange
1	teaspoon white wine vinegar

1. **To prepare the pâté,** preheat the oven to 350°F (180°C/gas 4). Butter a 9 x 5-inch (23 x 12-cm) loaf pan. Wrap in aluminum foil to make it waterproof.

2. **Cut** 5 ounces (150 g) of the salmon into small cubes. Chop the remaining 9 ounces (250 g) of salmon coarsely. Chop the eggs and coarsely chopped salmon in a food processor. Season with salt and pepper. Add the nutmeg and blend to make a smooth paste.

3. **Add** the spinach a little at a time, chopping until the mixture is smooth.

4. **Stir in** the cream and salmon cubes by hand. Spoon the mixture into the

prepared pan. Cover with aluminum foil. Place the pan in a baking pan half-filled with water.

5. **Bake** until set, about 1 hour. Remove from the oven and let cool. Chill overnight.

6. **To prepare the sauce,** bring the preserves, orange zest, orange juice, and vinegar to a boil over low heat. Simmer for 2–3 minutes. Discard the orange zest.

7. **Turn** the pâté out onto a serving dish. Slice thickly and serve with sauce spooned over the top.

If you liked this recipe, you will love these ones too:

ricotta mousse **with charred bell pepper sauce**
226

spinach **timbales**
240

spinach strudel with fruit chutney
260

crab cakes with roasted bell pepper sauce

Buy precooked crab meat for this dish, or use well-drained good quality canned crab meat. If using precooked crab meat, be sure to pick through it carefully to remove any pieces of shell.

Serves 6–8

15 minutes

30 minutes

1 hour

2

CRAB CAKES

1	tablespoon extra-virgin olive oil
1/2	red onion, finely chopped
1	stalk celery, finely diced
8	ounces (250 g) crabmeat
2	cups (120 g) soft white bread crumbs (no crusts)
2	tablespoons finely chopped fresh parsley
1	teaspoon finely chopped fresh thyme
1	scallion (spring onion), finely chopped
4	tablespoons (60 ml) mayonnaise
1	teaspoon Dijon mustard
1	large egg, lightly beaten
	Pinch of cayenne pepper
1/4	teaspoon Tabasco
1	tablespoon dry sherry
	Salt and freshly ground black pepper
3/4	cup (90 g) fine, dry bread crumbs

ROASTED BELL PEPPER SAUCE

3	red bell peppers (capsicums)
	Pinch of red pepper flakes
1	clove garlic, crushed
1/4	cup (45 g) toasted pine nuts
1	tablespoon freshly squeezed lemon juice
2–4	tablespoons extra-virgin olive oil
	Salt and freshly ground black pepper

1. To prepare the crab cakes, heat the oil in a large frying pan over medium heat. Add the onion and celery and sauté until softened, 3–4 minutes. Remove from the heat and let cool.

2. Combine the crabmeat, soft bread crumbs, parsley, thyme, scallion, mayonnaise, mustard, egg, cayenne pepper, Tabasco, sherry, salt, pepper, and onion mixture in a large bowl and mix well.

3. Lightly oil a large baking sheet. Form the crab mixture into cakes about 3 inches (9 cm) in diameter. Roll and pat the cakes in the dry bread crumbs to cover completely. Place on the baking sheet and refrigerate for 30 minutes.

4. To prepare the bell pepper sauce, preheat the broiler (grill) and roast the bell peppers until charred all over.

Place in a plastic bag and let rest for 10 minutes.

5. Remove the skins and seeds from the bell peppers. Chop in a food processor with the red pepper flakes, garlic, pine nuts, lemon juice, and 2 tablespoons of oil. Blend at high speed until smooth. If the mixture is too thick to blend properly, add a little more oil. Season with salt and pepper.

6. Place the baking sheet of chilled crab cakes under the hot broiler. Watch them carefully. Toast to golden brown on the top, then turn over and grill the other side until golden brown.

7. Serve the crab cakes hot with a dollop of the roasted bell pepper sauce spooned over each one.

thai fish cakes

Fish cakes are a delicious way to serve fish, especially to children or people who are not generally enthusiastic about seafood.

Serves 4

15 minutes

6–8 minutes

1

1	pound (500 g) boneless skinned white fish fillets, such as whiting, haddock, or snapper
1	large egg, lightly beaten
3	tablespoons Thai red curry paste
1	tablespoon Asian fish sauce
1	tablespoon cornstarch (cornflour)
2	scallions (spring onions), thinly sliced
2	tablespoons finely chopped fresh cilantro (coriander)
2	Kaffir lime leaves, finely shredded (optional)
	Vegetable oil, for frying

1. **Combine** the fish, egg, curry paste, fish sauce, and cornstarch in a food processor. Process until just combined.

2. **Stir in** the scallions, cilantro, and lime leaves, if using. Shape the mixture into twelve even-sized fish cakes.

3. **Heat** 1/2 inch (1 cm) of vegetable oil in a large frying pan or wok. Fry the fish cakes in batches, turning once, until golden and cooked through, 3–4 minutes on each side. Drain on paper towels and serve hot.

If you liked this recipe, you will love these ones too:

crab cakes **with roasted bell pepper sauce**

166

salmon **fish cakes**

170

salmon fish cakes

Serve these delicious fish cakes piping hot straight from the pan. For a lighter dish, bake the fish cakes in a hot oven until golden brown, about 20 minutes.

- Serves 4
- 10 minutes
- 1 hour
- 6–8 minutes
- 1

2	cups (400 g) canned pink salmon, drained and flaked
1½	cups (350 g) leftover mashed potatoes
2	scallions (spring onions), thinly sliced
2	tablespoons finely chopped fresh dill + extra, to garnish
1	large egg, lightly beaten

Salt and freshly ground black pepper
2 tablespoons all-purpose (plain) flour
¼ cup (60 ml) extra-virgin olive oil
Lemon wedges, to serve

1. **Mix** the salmon, mashed potatoes, scallions, dill, and egg in a large bowl. Season with salt and pepper. Shape the mixture into eight even-sized fish cakes. Lightly dust with the flour and chill in the refrigerator for 1 hour.

2. **Heat** the oil in a large frying pan over medium heat. Fry the fish cakes until golden brown, 3–4 minutes on each side. Drain on paper towels.

3. **Garnish** with the lemon wedges and extra dill and serve hot.

If you liked this recipe, you will love these ones too:

crab cakes **with roasted bell pepper sauce**

166

thai **fish cakes**

168

shrimp skewers

You will need about eight metal or bamboo skewers for this dish. If using bamboo skewers, be sure to soak them in cold water for 20 minutes or so before grilling.

Serves 4

25 minutes

1 hour

4–5 minutes

2

5	tablespoons (75 ml) extra virgin olive oil
1	pound (500 g) raw shrimp (green prawns), peeled and deveined
2	cloves garlic, finely chopped
4	tablespoons coarsely chopped fresh mint
	Salt and cracked pepper
1	cup (150 g) fine dry bread crumbs
	Lemon wedges, to serve

1. Put the oil in a medium bowl and add the shrimp. Toss to coat evenly. Add the garlic, mint, salt, and cracked pepper. Add the bread crumbs and toss lightly making sure all the shrimp are nicely coated. Cover and marinate for at least 1 hour in the refrigerator.

2. Preheat the overhead broiler (grill) in the oven. Thread 3–5 shrimp onto each skewer.

3. Place all the skewers on a lightly oiled baking sheet in the middle section of the oven under the broiler. Cook until the bread crumbs are golden and the shrimp have turned pick, about 2 minutes each side, depending on the size of the shrimp.

4. Drizzle with fresh lemon juice and serve hot.

If you liked this recipe, you will love these ones too:

shrimp & papaya **salad**

138

garlic **shrimp**

160

pan-fried squid with lemon

Make sure that the oil is very hot before adding each batch of squid. It needs to cook very quickly to avoid becoming soggy and chewy.

- Serves 6
- 20 minutes
- 15–20 minutes

1½	pounds (750 g) squid tubes
⅔	cup (100 g) fine semolina
1	teaspoon salt
1	teaspoon freshly ground black pepper

1	cup (250 ml) extra-virgin olive oil, to fry
1	lemon, cut into wedges

2

1. Cut each squid tube open along one side. With a sharp knife score inside the skin diagonally in both directions. Cut the squid into rectangles measuring about 1 x 2 inches (2 x 5 cm).

2. Combine the semolina, salt, and pepper in a small bowl.

3. Heat the oil in a large frying pan or wok over high heat. Dip the squid into the semolina mixture, turning to coat well and shaking off any excess.

4. Fry in small batches until crisp and golden brown, 3–4 minutes each batch. Drain on paper towels. Serve hot with the lemon wedges.

If you liked this recipe, you will love these ones too:

thai **fish cakes**
168

shrimp **skewers**
172

deep-fried **calamari** with almond crust
176

deep-fried calamari
with almond crust

Deep-fried calamari are always a treat but the almonds in the crust of this recipe add another dimension of crispness and flavor.

- Serves 4
- 15 minutes
- 20–25 minutes

- 2

½ cup (75 g) all-purpose (plain) flour

Salt and freshly ground black pepper

2 large eggs, lightly beaten

2 cups (300 g) fine dry bread crumbs

½ cup (50 g) finely chopped almonds

14 ounces (400 g) calamari (squid) bodies, cut in ¼-inch (5-mm) wide rings

4 cups (1 liter) oil, for frying

1 lemon, sliced, to garnish

1. **Combine** the flour, salt, and pepper in a bowl. Put the eggs in another bowl, and the bread crumbs and almonds in a third bowl.

2. **Roll** the calamari in the flour, shaking off any excess. Dip in the egg and roll in the bread crumbs and almonds.

3. **Heat** the frying oil in a large deep-fryer or deep saucepan until very hot.

Test the oil temperature by dropping in a small piece of bread. If it immediately bubbles to the surface and begins to turn golden, the oil is ready.

4. **Fry** the calamari in batches until crisp and golden brown, 5–7 minutes each batch. Drain on paper towels. Serve hot with the lemon.

If you liked this recipe, you will love these ones too:

crab cakes **with roasted bell pepper sauce**

166

shrimp **skewers**

172

pan-fried squid with lemon

174

Meat &
Chicken
Bites

salami with fresh figs

The simplest combinations of high quality, in-season ingredients often make the best dishes. Serve this elegant snack in late summer when the season's fresh figs arrive in the markets. The salty highly-spiced flavors of the salami blend beautifully with the sweet flesh of the figs.

- Serves 4–6
- 5 minutes

12	ounces (350 g) fresh green or black figs
5	ounces (150 g) thinly sliced salami, rinds removed

1

1. **Arrange** the figs and salami on a serving dish. If fresh fig leaves are available, place a layer on the serving dish before adding the figs and salami.

If you liked this recipe, you will love these ones too:

tuscan **bruschetta fingers**

32

prosciutto, peach & blue cheese **crostini**

40

brie & peach tartlets

60

stuffed fried olives

This is a traditional recipe from the Marches region of central Italy. The olives take some time and a little skill to make but they well are worth the effort!

Serves 8–10

40 minutes

40–50 minutes

3

2	tablespoons extra-virgin olive oil
5	ounces (150 g) ground (minced) beef
5	ounces (150 g) ground (minced) pork
2	tablespoons tomato paste (concentrate)
4	ounces (125 g) chicken livers, chopped
1	day-old bread roll
3	large eggs
5	tablespoons freshly grated Parmesan cheese

	Salt and freshly ground black pepper
	Dash of nutmeg
	Dash of cinnamon
60	giant green olives, pitted
1	cup (150 g) all-purpose (plain) flour
1	cup (150 g) fine dry bread crumbs
4	cups (1 liter) olive oil, for frying

1. Heat the extra-virgin olive oil in a medium-large frying pan over medium heat. Add the beef and pork and sauté until browned, about 5 minutes. Add the tomato paste and simmer over low heat for 15 minutes. Add the chicken livers and simmer for 5 minutes more.

2. Soak the bread roll in cold water, squeeze out excess moisture, and crumble.

3. Combine the meat mixture in a bowl with the bread, 1 egg, the Parmesan, salt, pepper, nutmeg, and cinnamon. Mix well.

4. Use this mixture to carefully stuff the olives one by one.

5. Set out three bowls, fill the first with the flour, the second with the remaining 2 eggs (beaten), and the third with the bread crumbs. Dredge the olives in the flour, dip them in the egg, and then in the bread crumbs.

6. Heat the frying oil in a deep-fryer or deep saucepan until very hot. Test the oil temperature by dropping in a small piece of bread. If it immediately bubbles to the surface and begins to turn golden, the oil is ready.

7. Fry the olives in small batches. When a crisp, golden crust forms around each olive, remove with a slotted spoon. Place on paper towels to drain. Serve hot.

sweet & spicy chicken wraps

Use leftover roast chicken to make these wraps or gently poach two chicken breasts in lightly salted simmering water until tender, 5–10 minutes.

- Serves 4
- 15 minutes
- 3–4 minutes
- 1

4	cups (400 g) shredded cooked chicken
⅓	cup (90 ml) mayonnaise
2	tablespoons Thai sweet chili sauce
4	Lebanese flat breads, pita breads, or flour tortillas
1	cucumber, thinly sliced
2	tomatoes, finely chopped
1	large carrot, finely grated
2	cups (100 g) finely shredded lettuce
	Salt and freshly ground black pepper

1. **Mix** the chicken, mayonnaise, and sweet chili sauce in a large clean bowl.

2. **Wrap** the flat breads or tortillas in barely damp double layers of paper towels and microwave on high for 45 seconds. Alternatively, heat them in a large ungreased frying pan over medium heat for 3–4 minutes.

3. **Lay** the flat breads out on a clean work surface. Divide the chicken mixture, cucumber, tomatoes, carrot, and lettuce evenly among the flat breads. Season with salt and pepper. Roll up and cut in half. Serve at once.

jamaican jerk **chicken wraps**
186

bagels **with turkey, cheese & cranberry sauce**
188

beef fajitas
190

jamaican jerk chicken wraps

This dish is named for the hot and spicy Jamaican spice mix used to flavor it. Jamaican Jerk spice mix is available in many ethnic food stores but if you can't find it you can improvise with a homemade mix of allspice, ground or crumbled chiles, ground cloves, cinnamon, nutmeg, thyme, garlic, salt, and pepper.

Serves 6

15 minutes

30 minutes

10–15 minutes

1

2	boneless skinless chicken breasts, cut into thin strips
2	red bell peppers (capsicums), seeded and cut into thin strips
1	red onion, thinly sliced
3	tablespoons Jamaican jerk spice mix
½	teaspoon cayenne pepper
1	tablespoon balsamic vinegar
3	tablespoons extra-virgin olive oil
1	tablespoon chile paste
6	large flour tortillas
5	ounces (150 g) freshly grated hard cheese, such as Cheddar or Gruyere

1. **Combine** the chicken, bell peppers, and onion in a medium bowl. Stir in the Jamaican jerk spice mix, cayenne, and balsamic vinegar. Mix well and chill for 30 minutes.

2. **Heat** the oil in a wok or deep-sided frying pan over low to medium heat and stir in the chile paste. Cook for a few seconds, stirring.

3. **Add** the chicken mixture and stir-fry until the chicken is cooked through, 10–15 minutes.

4. **Wrap** the tortillas in barely damp double layers of paper towels and microwave on high for 45 seconds. Alternatively, warm them in a large ungreased frying pan over medium heat for 3–4 minutes.

5. **Lay** the tortillas out and divide the chicken mixture among them. Top with the grated cheese. Roll up and serve hot.

sweet & spicy chicken wraps
184

bagels with turkey, cheese & cranberry sauce
188

steak sandwiches
194

bagels with turkey, cheese & cranberry sauce

If you can't get good New York-style bagels, use another small firm-textured bread for these sandwiches.

Serves 4

15 minutes

1

4	bagels, cut in half
1/3	cup (90 ml) cream cheese
8	slices roasted or seasoned cooked turkey breast
8	thin slices Camembert cheese
1/2	cup (120 ml) cranberry sauce
1	cup (60 g) pea shoots or snow pea sprouts
	Salt and freshly ground black pepper

1. **Wrap** the bagels in barely damp double layers of paper towels and microwave on high for 45 seconds. Alternatively, warm them in a large ungreased frying pan over medium heat for 3–4 minutes.

2. **Put** the bagel halves on a clean work surface. Spread each half with the cream cheese. Top evenly with the turkey, Camembert, cranberry sauce, and pea shoots. Season with salt and pepper and serve warm.

If you liked this recipe, you will love these ones too:

sweet & spicy **chicken wraps**

184

jamaican **chicken wraps**

186

classic beef burgers

192

beef fajitas

Fajitas come from Tex-Mex cuisine and the term originally referred to grilled beef wrapped in a warm tortilla. Nowadays many different meats are served in this away with a wide variety of sauces and seasonings.

- Serves 4
- 15 minutes
- 30 minutes
- 15 minutes
- 1

1	pound (500 g) lean beef strips, cut from the rump
1	teaspoon sweet paprika
1	teaspoon ground cumin
1	teaspoon ground coriander
½	teaspoon chile powder
¼	cup (60 ml) freshly squeezed lime juice
4	tablespoons (60 ml) extra-virgin olive oil
2	onions, thinly sliced
1	red bell pepper (capsicum), seeded and thinly sliced
8	large flour tortillas
	Fresh cilantro (coriander) leaves, to serve
	Sour cream, to serve

1. Mix the beef, paprika, cumin, coriander, chile powder, and lime juice in a large bowl. Cover with plastic wrap (cling film) and marinate in the refrigerator for 30 minutes.

2. Meanwhile, heat 2 tablespoons of oil in a large frying pan over medium-high. Add the onions and bell pepper and sauté until softened, about 5 minutes. Remove and set aside.

3. Add the remaining 2 tablespoons of oil to the same frying pan. Add the beef and sauté until browned, about 5 minutes. Add the onion and bell pepper mixture. Sauté for 2–3 minutes.

4. Wrap the tortillas in barely damp double layers of paper towels and microwave on high for 45 seconds. Alternatively, warm them in a large ungreased frying pan over medium heat for 3–4 minutes.

5. Lay the tortillas out on a work surface and cover with the beef mixture. Top with cilantro and sour cream, roll up, and serve hot.

jamaican jerk **chicken wraps**

186

classic beef burgers

192

steak sandwiches

194

classic beef burgers

Making hamburgers at home is a sure way to please everyone. It also allows you to use fresh, high-quality ingredients so that this fast food classic becomes a healthy snack.

Serves 6

15 minutes

20 minutes

1

1	cup (60 g) fresh white bread crumbs
1	pound (500 g) ground (minced) beef
2	tablespoons tomato ketchup + extra, to serve
2	teaspoons mixed dried herbs
1	large egg, lightly beaten

	Salt and freshly ground black pepper
2	tablespoons extra-virgin olive oil
2	onions, thinly sliced
4	hamburger buns, cut in half
1	small lettuce
1	large tomato, thinly sliced

1. **Mix** the bread crumbs, beef, tomato ketchup, mixed herbs, and egg in a large bowl. Season with salt and pepper. Divide the mixture into four and shape into burgers.

2. **Place** a grill pan over medium-high heat. Drizzle with oil. Grill the onions until golden, about 10 minutes. Set aside.

3. **Grill** the burgers until cooked, about 5 minutes on each side. Lightly toast the buns on the grill.

4. **Fill** the buns with the lettuce, tomato, burgers, and onion. Top with tomato ketchup and sandwich together. Serve hot.

beef fajitas

190

steak sandwiches

194

steak sandwiches

Serve this hearty, high-protein snack to hungry skiers during a day on the slopes or to other sportsmen and women (or girls and boys). It will provide them with plenty of energy.

Serves 4

15 minutes

10–15 minutes

1

2 tablespoons extra-virgin olive oil
2 red onions, thinly sliced
2 beef tenderloins (fillet steaks)
2 cloves garlic, finely chopped
2 baguettes (French loaves), halved lengthwise

1 cup (50 g) arugula (rocket)
2 tomatoes, thickly sliced
Salt and freshly ground black pepper
Barbecue sauce, to serve

1. **Heat** 1 tablespoon of oil in a large frying pan over medium heat. Add the onions and sauté until softened, 3–4 minutes. Set aside.

2. **Heat** the remaining 1 tablespoon of oil in the same pan over medium-high heat. Sauté the steak with the garlic until cooked to your liking, about 4 minutes on each side. Cut each steak in half lengthwise.

3. **Fill** the baguettes with the arugula, tomatoes, steak, and onions. Season with salt and pepper. Drizzle with the barbecue sauce.

4. **Cut** each baguette in half and serve while the steak is still warm.

jamaican jerk **chicken wraps**
186

beef **fajitas**
190

classic beef burgers
192

baked chicken & coconut meatballs

This recipe makes 24 chicken balls. If preparing for a larger group or a party buffet, just double or triple the recipe as required. Prepare the balls ahead of time and bake just before serving.

Serves 4–6

15 minutes

15–20 minutes

1

1	pound (500 g) ground (minced) chicken
1/4	cup (60 ml) Thai chili sauce + extra to serve
2	cloves garlic, finely chopped
1	teaspoon finely chopped fresh ginger

1	tablespoon Thai fish sauce
1/2	cup (25 g) finely chopped fresh cilantro (coriander) leaves
2/3	cup (150 ml) coconut milk Salt and freshly ground black peper

1. Preheat the oven to 400°F (200°C/gas 6). Lightly oil two 12-cup mini muffin tins.

2. Combine the chicken, chili sauce, garlic, ginger, fish sauce, cilantro, and coconut milk in a medium bowl. Season with salt and pepper and mix well.

3. Spoon the mixture into the prepared muffins tins.

4. Bake until golden brown and cooked through, 15–20 minutes. Serve hot with extra chili sauce.

If you liked this recipe, you will love these ones too:

pilotas

210

stuffed kibbe

212

fiery meatballs

214

croquettes with ham & cheese

Serve these high-energy snacks hot with a green salad. They provide enough energy to count as a complete meal.

- Serves 4–6
- 15 minutes
- 15–20 minutes
- 2

¼ cup (60 g) butter
1 cup (150 g) all-purpose (plain) flour
1⅓ cups (320 ml) milk
½ meat stock cube, crumbled
⅓ cup (50 g) freshly grated Gruyère cheese
4 ounces (125 g) ham, chopped

Pinch of freshly grated nutmeg
2 large eggs, separated
1 cup (150 g) fine dry bread crumbs
4 cups (1 liter) vegetable oil, for frying

1. Melt the butter in a saucepan over low heat. Add ⅔ cup (100 g) of flour and mix well. Remove from the heat and add the milk and stock cube, mixing to prevent lumps forming.

2. Return to the heat and bring to a boil, stirring constantly. Cook until thick and creamy, 3–4 minutes. Add the cheese, ham, and nutmeg. Mix well and remove from the heat. Stir in 1 egg yolk and let cool. Beat the remaining eggs in a small bowl.

3. Put the remaining ⅓ cup (50 g) flour on a plate. Put the bread crumbs on a second plate. Shape walnut-sized croquettes from the cheese mixture using your hands. Dredge in the flour, dip in the beaten egg, and roll in the bread crumbs.

4. Heat the frying oil in a deep-fryer or deep saucepan until very hot. Test the oil temperature by dropping in a small piece of bread. If it immediately bubbles to the surface and begins to turn golden, the oil is ready.

5. Fry the croquettes in batches until golden brown all over, about 5 minutes each batch. Scoop out with a slotted spoon and drain on paper towels. Serve hot.

If you liked this recipe, you will love these ones too:

stuffed fried **olives**

182

stuffed rice **croquettes**

200

stuffed **kibbe**

212

stuffed rice croquettes

This is another classic Italian snack or appetizer. The recipe comes from Lazio, where it is known as *Suppli alla romana*. Serve hot straight from the pan.

Serves 6–8

15 minutes

1 hour

40–50 minutes

3

4	tablespoons (60 ml) extra-virgin olive oil	
2	cups (400 g) short-grain rice, such as Arborio	
4	cups (1 liter) beef stock	
1	small onion, chopped	
4	ounces (125 g) chicken livers, coarsely chopped	
2	ounces (60 g) ground (minced) veal	
1	cup (150 g) frozen peas	
2	tablespoons white wine	
1	large tomato, peeled and chopped	

Salt and freshly ground black pepper

2 tablespoons freshly grated Parmesan cheese

2 tablespoons butter

2 hard-boiled eggs, peeled and chopped

2 raw eggs

1⅓ cups (200 g) fine dry bread crumbs

4 cups (1 liter) oil, for frying

1. **Heat** 2 tablespoons of oil in a large frying pan over medium-high heat. Add the rice and stir for 2 minutes to toast. Begin adding the stock a ladleful at a time, cooking and stirring until it has all been absorbed and the rice is tender. The cooking method is similar to making a risotto. It will take 15–20 minutes for the rice to be cooked. Remove from the heat and set aside to cool for 1 hour.

2. **Heat** the remaining 2 tablespoons of oil in a medium frying pan over medium heat. Add the onion and sauté until softened, 3–4 minutes.

3. **Add** the chicken livers, veal, peas, and wine and simmer until the wine has evaporated, about 5 minutes. Add the tomato and season with salt and pepper. Continue cooking, stirring often, until the sauce is thick and well cooked, about 20 minutes.

4. **Combine** the cooled rice, Parmesan, and butter in a bowl. Mix well and mold into round croquettes about the size of golf balls. Hollow out the center of each croquette and fill with meat sauce and a piece of hard-boiled egg. Close the rice around the filling.

5. **Beat** the raw eggs with a fork in a shallow dish. Dip the croquettes into the egg and then roll in bread crumbs.

6. **Heat** the frying oil in a deep-fryer or deep saucepan until very hot. Test the oil temperature by dropping in a small piece of bread. If it immediately bubbles to the surface and begins to turn golden, the oil is ready.

7. **Fry** the croquettes in batches until crisp and golden brown, about 5 minutes each batch. Scoop out with a slotted spoon and drain on paper towels. Serve hot.

ham pâté

For a lighter dish, use reduced-fat mascarpone or cream cheese.

Serves 6

15 minutes

4–12 hours

1

8 ounces (250 g) ham, chopped
3 ounces (90 g) fresh ricotta cheese, drained
8 ounces (250 g) mascarpone or cream cheese
2 tablespoons brandy
Freshly grated nutmeg

Salt and freshly ground black pepper
4 walnuts, to decorate
2 tablespoons pine nuts
Warm toast, to serve

1. Butter 6 small ramekins and line with plastic wrap (cling film).

2. Combine the ham, ricotta, mascarpone, brandy, and nutmeg in the bowl of a food processor. Season with salt and pepper and blend to make a smooth paste.

3. Spoon the mixture into the ramekins. Chill in the refrigerator for 4 hours or overnight.

4. Turn the pâté out onto serving dishes and carefully remove the plastic wrap.

5. Decorate with walnuts and pine nuts. Serve with warm toasted bread.

If you liked this recipe, you will love these ones too:

chicken liver & orange **pâté**

204

rustic **pâté**

206

liver **pâté**

208

chicken liver & orange pâté

If desired, reduce the amount of orange juice to $1/4$ cup (60 ml) and add 2 tablespoons of Grand Marnier.

- Serves 6–8
- 15 minutes
- 4–12 hours
- 10–15 minutes
- 2

12	ounces (350 g) salted butter, softened
1	shallot, chopped
12	ounces (350 g) chicken livers, chopped
	Salt and freshly ground black pepper

$1/3$ cup (90 ml) freshly squeezed orange juice

Thinly sliced orange, to garnish

Fresh bread or toast, to serve

1. Butter 6–8 small ramekins.
2. Heat 2 tablespoons of butter in a frying pan over medium heat. Add the shallot and sauté until softened, 3–4 minutes.
3. Add the chicken livers and sauté until cooked through, about 7 minutes. Season with salt and pepper.
4. Transfer to a food processor and blend until smooth. Add the orange juice and remaining butter and blend until smooth.
5. Spoon the mixture into the ramekins and chill for 4 hours or overnight.
6. Turn the pâté out onto serving dishes. Garnish with slices of orange. Serve with fresh bread or warm toast.

If you liked this recipe, you will love these ones too:

tuscan chicken liver **crostini**

54

ham **pâté**

202

liver **pâté**

208

rustic pâté

This pretty pâté takes some time and skill to prepare and chill. It is perfect for buffet parties and special occasions. Serve in slices with plenty of fresh bread or warm toast.

Serves 8–12

15 minutes

24 hours

1 1/2 hours

3

1	pound (500 g) pork loin, finely chopped
14	ounces (400 g) pig liver, finely chopped
8	ounces (250 g) lard or bacon fat, finely chopped
1	large onion, finely chopped
1	clove garlic, finely chopped
1	tablespoon green peppercorns preserved in brine, rinsed and drained
12	black peppercorns
1/4	teaspoon freshly grated nutmeg
	Salt

1/3	cup (90 ml) Calvados (apple brandy)
2	bay leaves
4	cloves
1 1/2	cups (375 ml) water
1	tablespoon powdered gelatin
1	piece bottled roasted red bell pepper (capsicum), drained and sliced, to garnish
3	mushrooms preserved in oil, sliced, to garnish
	Leaves from 1 sprig parsley

1. Preheat the oven to 350°F (180°C/ gas 4). Oil a 5 x 9-inch (12 x 23-cm) loaf pan.

2. Place the pork loin and liver in a large bowl. Add the lard, onion, garlic, green peppercorns, black peppercorns, nutmeg, and salt. Stir in the Calvados then mix well using your hands.

3. Transfer the mixture to the prepared pan and smooth the surface using the back of a spoon. Top with the bay leaves and cloves.

4. Bake until the meat is cooked through and the top is lightly browned, about 90 minutes.

5. Remove from the oven and drain the juices into a large saucepan. Skim off any fat and discard it. Let cool completely.

6. Put the water in the saucepan. Add the gelatin and mix well. Bring to a boil over low heat, stirring until the gelatin has completely dissolved. Remove from the heat and let cool.

7. Pour the gelatin mixture over the pâté. Cover and chill in the refrigerator for 24 hours.

8. Turn the pâté out onto a serving dish. Turn right-side up and decorate with the bell pepper, mushrooms, and parsley. Slice and serve.

liver pâté

This classic liver pâté can be served as is with fresh bread or toast, but it is also delicious in sandwiches with salad greens and sliced tomatoes.

Serves 6

30 minutes

4–12 hours

45–50 minutes

2

6	tablespoons (90 g) butter
1	onion, finely chopped
12	ounces (350 g) calf's liver, chopped
8	ounces (250 g) lard, chopped
1	tablespoon finely chopped fresh parsley

1	tablespoon finely chopped fresh tarragon
½	cup (75 g) all-purpose (plain) flour
2	large eggs
	Dash of nutmeg
	Salt and freshly ground white pepper

1. **Preheat** the oven to 350°F (180°C/gas 4).

2. **Heat** 1 tablespoon of butter in a small saucepan over medium heat. Add the onion and sauté for 3–4 minutes. When it begins to turn golden, turn off the heat and add the remaining butter so it melts without bubbling.

3. **Put** the liver and lard in the bowl of a food processor and add the onion mixture, parsley, and tarragon. Chop finely. Add the flour, eggs, nutmeg, salt, and pepper, and mix thoroughly by hand.

4. **Butter** a small loaf pan, line with aluminum foil, and fill with the mixture. Shake the mold to fill up any air pockets. Cover with a sheet of foil.

5. **Place** the mold in a large baking pan. Pour in enough boiling water to come halfway up the sides of the loaf pan. Bake for 45–50 minutes, until cooked through.

6. **Let cool** to room temperature then chill in the refrigerator for 4 hours or overnight. Slice and serve.

If you liked this recipe, you will love these ones too:

ham **pâté**

202

chicken liver & orange **pâté**

204

rustic **pâté**

206

pilotas

These tasty little meatballs come from the Catalan region of Spain. They are best when eaten hot, and can be prepared ahead of time and cooked just before serving.

Serves 4–6

10 minutes

5–10 minutes

1

1	pound (500 g) ground (minced) pork
1	cup (50 g) fresh bread crumbs
2	large eggs, lightly beaten
2	tablespoons finely chopped fresh parsley
3	cloves garlic, finely chopped

⅓	cup (50 g) pine nuts
	Salt and freshly ground black pepper
½	teaspoon ground cinnamon
½	teaspoon ground nutmeg
½	cup (125 ml) olive oil, for frying

1. **Place** the pork in a large bowl and stir in the bread crumbs, eggs, parsley, garlic, pine nuts, salt, pepper, cinnamon, and nutmeg. Mix well.

2. **Heat** the oil in a large frying pan over medium-high heat and fry the pilotas until golden brown all over, 5–10 minutes.

3. **Place** the cooked pilotas on a preheated plate covered with paper towels to drain. Serve hot.

If you liked this recipe, you will love these ones too:

stuffed **kibbe**

212

fiery **meatballs**

214

meatballs with sage butter

216

stuffed kibbe

Kibbe are a type of Middle Eastern meatball made from a mixture of spiced bulgur and meat.

Serves 12–15

25 minutes

1 hour

30–35 minutes

2

KIBBE

2	pounds (1 kg) fine-grind bulgur
2	pounds (1 kg) ground (minced) beef
1	large onion, finely chopped
½	teaspoon freshly grated nutmeg
½	teaspoon ground cinnamon
	Salt and freshly ground black pepper

FILLING

¼	cup (60 ml) extra-virgin olive oil
4	medium onions, finely chopped
1	pound (500 g) ground (minced) lamb
	Salt
½	teaspoon ground cinnamon
½	teaspoon ground allspice
4	cups (1 liter) olive or sesame oil, for frying

1. **To prepare the kibbe,** put the bulgur in a bowl and cover with cold water. Let stand for 30 minutes. Drain well.

2. **Mix** the beef and onion in a large bowl. Stir in the bulgur, nutmeg, and cinnamon. Season with salt and pepper. Use your hands to knead the mixture until well mixed. Shape into a ball, return to the bowl, and refrigerate for 30 minutes.

3. **To prepare the filling,** heat the oil in a large frying pan over medium heat. Sauté the onions until lightly browned, about 5 minutes. Add the lamb and season with salt, cinnamon, and allspice. Simmer until the meat is browned, about 10 minutes. Remove from the heat and set aside.

4. **Use** a tablespoon to scoop out enough of the bulgur mixture to form balls the size of golf balls. Use your index finger to make a hollow in the center. Spoon in the filling and close up the opening. Repeat until both mixtures are all used up.

5. **Heat** the frying oil in a deep-fryer or deep saucepan until very hot. Test the oil temperature by dropping in a small piece of bread. If it immediately bubbles to the surface and begins to turn golden, the oil is ready.

6. **Fry** the kibbe in batches until golden brown all over, 5–7 minutes per batch. Drain on paper towels. Serve hot.

fiery meatballs

You can experiment with the ingredients in these spicy meatballs, adding more chiles and fresh herbs, such as mint, sage, lemon balm, rosemary, and dill or using ground lamb with cumin, turmeric, and cilantro for a different taste.

Serves 4–6

15 minutes

15 minutes

10–15 minutes

1

2	tablespoons extra-virgin olive oil
1	large onion, finely chopped
2	large cloves garlic, thinly sliced
14	ounces (400 g) ground (minced) beef
8	ounces (250 g) ground (minced) pork
2	small hot chiles, seeded and finely chopped
½	teaspoon salt
¼	teaspoon coarsely ground black pepper
½	teaspoon strong mustard

1	teaspoon hot smoked paprika
¾	inch (2 cm) fresh ginger, peeled and grated
2	tablespoons fine dry bread crumbs
1	tablespoon freshly grated Parmesan cheese
2	tablespoons finely chopped fresh parsley
1	large egg, beaten
	Salt and freshly ground black pepper
3	tablespoons sunflower oil

1. **Heat** the olive oil in a large frying pan over medium heat. Add the onion and garlic and sauté until softened, 3–4 minutes.

2. **Mix** the beef and pork in a large bowl and add the onion and garlic mixture. Stir in the chiles, salt, pepper, mustard, paprika, ginger, bread crumbs, Parmesan, and parsley and mix well.

3. **Add** the egg and mix thoroughly using your hands. Taste for seasoning. Set aside for 15 minutes.

4. **Moisten** your hands and shape the mixture into about 20 small meatballs.

5. Heat the sunflower oil in a large frying pan over medium-high heat. Fry the meatballs until golden and cooked through, 5–10 minutes. Serve hot.

If you liked this recipe, you will love these ones too:

pilotas

210

stuffed kibbe

212

meatballs with sage butter

216

meatballs with sage butter

These meatballs can be served hot and also at room temperature, making them ideal for a buffet spread or to take on a picnic.

Serves 6

15 minutes

25–30 minutes

1

2	cups (100 g) fresh bread crumbs	
¼	cup (60 ml) milk	
1½	pounds (750 g) lean ground (minced) beef	
1	large egg, lightly beaten	
2	tablespoons finely chopped fresh parsley	
	Salt and freshly ground black pepper	

6	ounces (180 g) Fontina or other mild firm cheese, cut into small cubes
¼	cup (30 g) all-purpose (plain) flour
¼	cup (60 g) butter
1	sprig fresh sage
½	cup (125 ml) dry white wine

1. Drizzle the bread crumbs with the milk in a small bowl. Combine the meat in a large bowl with the bread crumbs, egg, and parsley. Season with salt and pepper and mix well.

2. Shape the mixture into meatballs the size of large walnuts. Push a piece of cheese into the center of each one, closing the meat over the cheese and sealing well.

3. Place the flour on a plate and dredge each meatball in it. Shake gently to remove excess flour.

4. Melt the butter in a large saucepan over medium heat. Add the sage and meatballs. Sauté until browned all over, about 5 minutes. Add the wine and simmer it evaporates.

5. Lower the heat, cover, and simmer until the meatballs are tender and cooked through, about 20 minutes.

6. Place on a serving dish and drizzle with the cooking juices. Garnish with the sprig of sage and serve hot or at room temperature.

If you liked this recipe, you will love these ones too:

stuffed rice croquettes

200

pilotas

210

stuffed kibbe

212

lamb kebabs with tzatziki

These kebabs make wonderful barbecue food. They can be prepared the day before and chilled until just before cooking. If using bamboo skewers, be sure to soak them in cold water for about 30 minutes before use so that they don't burn during cooking.

Serves 4–8

45 minutes

12 hours

10 minutes

1

KEBABS

12	ounces (350 g) ground (minced) lamb
1	cup (60 g) fresh bread crumbs
1	clove garlic, finely chopped
1	small onion, finely chopped
1	teaspoon ground cumin
1	tablespoon finely chopped fresh parsley
1	tablespoon finely chopped fresh mint
1	teaspoon finely chopped fresh oregano
	Finely grated zest of 1 lemon
1	large egg
	Salt and freshly ground black pepper

TZATZIKI

1	cucumber
1	cup (250 ml) thick Greek-style yogurt
2	cloves garlic, finely chopped
1	bunch fresh mint, finely chopped
2	tablespoons extra-virgin olive oil
1	tablespoon white wine vinegar
	Salt and freshly ground black pepper

1. **To prepare the kebabs,** mix the lamb, bread crumbs, garlic, onion, cumin, parsley, mint, oregano, lemon zest, and egg in a large bowl. Season with salt and pepper.

2. **Roll** the mixture into sausage shapes and thread onto eight bamboo or metal skewers. Arrange the kebabs on a tray and chill overnight in the refrigerator.

3. **Oil** a grill rack or grill pan and grill the kebabs, turning frequently, until golden brown and cooked to your liking, about 10 minutes.

4. **To prepare the tzatziki,** peel the cucumber. Cut it in half and scoop out the seeds. Cut into very small dice. Sprinkle with salt and drain in a colander for 10 minutes. Squeeze out the excess moisture.

5. **Mix** the yogurt, garlic, cucumber, and mint in a large bowl. Stir in the oil and vinegar and season with salt and pepper.

6. **Serve** the kebabs hot with the tzatziki.

Garden
Fresh

tomato sorbet

This unusual snack is perfect on a hot summer's day. Be sure not to use overripe tomatoes; you need firm, just-ripe tomatoes, preferably plucked fresh from the vine.

Serves 6–8

25 minutes

About 1 hour

5–10 minutes

2

2	pounds (1 kg) firm, ripe tomatoes
½	cup (100 g) sugar
2	cups (500 ml) water
	Freshly squeezed juice of 1 lemon

Salt
Fresh basil leaves, to garnish

1. Blanch the tomatoes in boiling water for 30 seconds. Drain well. Transfer to a food processor and process until smooth.

2. Strain the tomato mixture through a fine-mesh sieve to remove the skins and seeds.

3. Mix the sugar and water in a medium saucepan. Bring to a boil and simmer over low heat until the sugar has dissolved and the syrup is clear.

Remove from the heat and let cool to room temperature, about 30 minutes.

4. Mix in the strained tomato juice and lemon juice. Season with salt.

5. Pour the mixture into an ice-cream machine and freeze according to the manufacturer's instructions.

6. Spoon into individual serving dishes or glasses and freeze for 10 minutes. Garnish with sprigs of basil and serve.

If you liked this recipe, you will love these ones too:

strawberry & champagne **granita**

284

kiwi **sorbet**

286

melon **sorbet** with orange & basil

288

cheese & celery snacks

This light and healthy snack is perfect in the warm summer months. If you don't like the strong flavor of the garlic, just leave it out.

Serves 4

15 minutes

1 hour

15 minutes

1

8	ounces (250 g) fresh ricotta cheese, drained
4	ounces (125 g) blue cheese, crumbled into small pieces
¼	cup (60 g) milk or sour cream
2	cloves garlic, finely chopped
1	tablespoon finely chopped fresh chives

1	tablespoon extra-virgin olive oil
	Salt and freshly ground black pepper
10	large stalks very fresh celery
1	tablespoon finely chopped fresh parsley

1. **Put** the ricotta in a bowl. Add the blue cheese and milk and mash until smooth and creamy. Add the garlic, chives, oil, salt, and pepper, mixing well.

2. **Cover** and chill in the refrigerator for 1 hour.

3. **Trim** the celery stalks and remove any tough external fibers. Cut into pieces about 3 inches (8 cm) long.

4. **Fill** the celery with the cheese mixture, sprinkle with the parsley, and serve.

If you liked this recipe, you will love these ones too:

ricotta mousse **with charred bell pepper sauce**
226

eggplant & bell pepper **salad**
228

fennel salad
230

ricotta mousse
with charred bell pepper sauce

This is a striking dish with delicious flavors. Use red bell peppers for a different colored sauce.

Serves 4–6

25 minutes

4 hours

15 minutes

2

1	teaspoon gelatin powder
2	tablespoons boiling water
2	tablespoons freshly squeezed lemon juice
14	ounces (400 g) fresh ricotta cheese, drained
½	cup (125 ml) milk
2	cups (100 g) watercress, chopped + extra, to garnish

4	scallions (green onions), finely chopped
	Salt and freshly ground black pepper
2	large yellow peppers (capsicums)
1	clove garlic, chopped
¼	cup (60 ml) extra-virgin olive oil

1. **Butter** 4–6 small ramekins. Dissolve the gelatin in the boiling water in a cup or small bowl. Add the lemon juice and mix well.

2. **Press** the ricotta through a fine-mesh sieve. Mix the milk and ricotta in a large bowl. Add the watercress, scallions, and gelatin mixture. Season with salt and pepper.

3. **Spoon** the mixture into the ramekins and chill for 4 hours.

4. **Preheat** the overhead oven broiler (grill) on medium-high. Broil the bell peppers until charred all over. Place in a plastic bag. Seal the bag and let rest for 15 minutes.

5. **Remove** the bell peppers from the bag. Peel and remove the seeds. Chop in a food processor with the garlic and oil until smooth. Season with salt and pepper.

6. **Spoon** the bell pepper cream onto four to six serving dishes. Turn the mousses out onto the sauce. Garnish with watercress and serve.

If you liked this recipe, you will love these ones too:

cheese & celery **snacks**

224

artichoke hearts **stuffed with cheese**

236

fried mozzarella

280

eggplant & bell pepper salad

Use only the freshest, locally grown eggplant and bell peppers for this dish.

Serves 4

10 minutes

30 minutes

20–25 minutes

1

SALAD

1	red bell pepper (capsicum)
4	medium eggplants (aubergines)
1/4	cup (60 ml) extra-virgin olive oil

DRESSING

3	tablespoons extra-virgin olive oil
2	tablespoons freshly squeezed lemon juice
2	cloves garlic, crushed
	Salt
1/2	teaspoon paprika
1/4	teaspoon cayenne pepper
2	tablespoons finely chopped fresh flat-leaf parsley

1. **To prepare the salad,** slice off the four sides of the bell pepper (capsicum) and trim off the curved ends so the pieces are flat. Brush the skin side with oil.

2. **Preheat** the overhead oven broiler (grill) on medium-high. Broil the bell peppers skin-side up until the skin is blackened and blistered. Transfer to a plastic bag, seal, and let sweat for 15 minutes.

3. **Remove** the stems from the eggplants. Peel off 1/2-inch (1-cm) wide strips of skin lengthwise at intervals to create a striped effect. Slice into rounds 1/4 inch (5 mm) thick. Set aside.

4. **Brush** both sides of the eggplant with oil. Broil (grill) on both sides until browned and cooked through. Place on a serving platter.

5. **Peel** the bell pepper slices and cut into small squares. Arrange on top of the eggplant.

6. **To prepare the dressing,** whisk the oil, lemon juice, garlic, salt, paprika, cayenne, and parsley in a small bowl. Drizzle over the eggplants. Let stand for 15 minutes before serving.

If you liked this recipe, you will love these ones too:

roasted bell peppers **with anchovies**
238

neapolitan **crêpes**
246

ratatouille tart
256

fennel salad

Fennel has a refreshing, light anise flavor. It is a good source of dietary fiber, folate, and potassium and is believed to have anticancer and anti-inflammatory properties as well being an aid for digestion.

Serves 4

5–10 minutes

1

2	fennel bulbs
2	tablespoons extra-virgin olive oil
1	tablespoon freshly squeezed lemon juice
2	tablespoons finely chopped fresh parsley
1	tablespoon snipped fresh chives
	Salt and freshly ground black pepper

1. **Slice** the fennel bulbs crosswise into thin slices. Separate the rings and arrange them in a salad bowl.

2. **Whisk** the oil, lemon juice, parsley, chives, salt, and pepper in a small bowl.

3. **Drizzle** the dressing over the fennel, toss gently, and serve at once.

If you liked this recipe, you will love these ones too:

cheese & celery **snacks**

224

summer potato **salad**

232

goat cheese & fruit salad

234

summer potato salad

This dish makes a nutritious snack or light lunch. Serve with slices of freshly baked bread.

Serves 4–6

20 minutes

30 minutes

20 minutes

1

2	pounds (1 kg) waxy potatoes
1	medium onion, thinly sliced
¼	cup (60 ml) cold water
1	tablespoon white wine vinegar
	Salt
8	ounces (250 g) canned tuna, drained
2	cucumbers, thinly sliced
1	cup (100 g) mixed black and green olives

2	tablespoons extra-virgin olive oil
1	tomato, cut in wedges
3	hard-boiled eggs, quartered
8	anchovy fillets
1	yellow bell pepper (capsicum), seeded, cored, and cut into thin strips
	Fresh parsley leaves, to garnish

1. **Cook** the potatoes in their skins in a large pot of salted, boiling water until tender, about 20 minutes.

2. **Slip the skins off** the potatoes and let cool completely. Cut into bite-size pieces.

3. **Place** the onion in a large bowl with the water, vinegar, and 1 teaspoon salt. Let stand for 30 minutes. Drain well.

4. **Combine** the potatoes, tuna, cucumbers, olives, and onion in a large salad bowl. Season with salt and drizzle with the oil.

5. **Toss gently** and garnish with the tomato, egg, anchovies, bell pepper, and parsley. Serve at once.

If you liked this recipe, you will love these ones too:

eggplant & bell pepper **salad**

228

fennel **salad**

230

goat cheese & fruit salad

234

goat cheese & fruit salad

Amaze your guests with this pretty summer salad.

Serves 6

25 minutes

1

5	ounces (150 g) soft creamy goat cheese, such as chèvre or caprino
4	tablespoons finely chopped mixed fresh herbs (parsley, chives, mint, thyme, basil, marjoram, tarragon, dill)
1	small cantaloupe (rock) melon, about 12 ounces (350 g)
1	large cucumber, peeled

	Freshly squeezed juice of 1 orange
	Salt
12	cherry tomatoes
6	small radishes, trimmed
4	tablespoons (60 ml) extra-virgin olive oil
5	ounces (150 g) purple grapes
	Fresh baby spinach leaves

1. **Shape** the goat cheese into marble-size balls. Roll them in a dish filled with the herbs until well coated. Set aside.

2. **Use** a melon baller to make balls from the melon and cucumber. Sprinkle the melon balls with 1 tablespoon of orange juice. Drizzle the cucumber balls with 1 tablespoon of oil and season with salt.

3. **Line** a large serving bowl with fresh spinach leaves. Arrange the cheese, vegetables, and fruit on top.

4. **Drizzle** with the remaining 3 tablespoons (45 ml) of oil and orange juice. Toss gently and serve.

If you liked this recipe, you will love these ones too:

pear & hazelnut **crostoni**

34

prosciutto, peach & blue cheese **crostini**

40

cheese & celery **snacks**

224

artichoke hearts
stuffed with cheese

Artichokes are packed with fiber and phytochemicals that are believed to help the liver and fight against cholesterol.

Serves 4

10 minutes

2–3 minutes

1

1	pound (500 g) jar or can artichoke hearts, drained
1	cup (250 g) fresh ricotta cheese, drained
2	tablespoons finely chopped red bell pepper (capsicum)
1	tablespoon finely chopped fresh parsley
$\frac{1}{2}$	teaspoon black cracked pepper
4	tablespoons freshly grated Parmesan cheese

1. **Slice** the bottoms off the artichoke hearts so they will stand upright.

2. **Combine** the ricotta, bell pepper, parsley, and pepper in a small bowl and mix well.

3. **Spoon** some of the mixture into the center of each artichoke heart. Sprinkle with the Parmesan.

4. **Preheat** the overhead oven broiler (grill) to medium-high. Broil the artichoke hearts until the cheese begins to turn golden, 2–3 minutes. Serve warm.

If you liked this recipe, you will love these ones too:

cheese & celery **snacks**

224

ricotta mousse **with charred bell pepper sauce**

226

fried parmesan puffs

278

roasted bell peppers
with anchovies

Bell peppers, also known as capsicums and peppers, are a good source of vitamin C. For best results, prepare this dish the day before serving and chill overnight in the refrigerator. Take out about one hour before serving.

- Serves 8
- 30 minutes
- 2 hours
- 20–30 minutes

- 2

2	yellow bell peppers (capsicums)
2	green bell peppers (capsicums)
2	red bell peppers (capsicums)
8	anchovy fillets
4	cloves garlic, finely chopped
4	tablespoons finely chopped fresh parsley
2	tablespoons brine-cured capers, drained
1/2	teaspoon dried oregano
4	tablespoons (60 ml) extra-virgin olive oil
2	tablespoons coarsely chopped fresh basil leaves

1. **Preheat** the oven to 400°F (200°C/gas 6). Slice the bell peppers in half lengthwise. Remove the seeds and pulpy core. Rinse under cold running water and shake dry.

2. **Bake** in the oven, skin-side up, until the skins are blistered and black, 20–30 minutes. Place in a plastic bag and leave to sweat for 15 minutes.

3. **Remove** the charred skins from the bell peppers with your fingers. Cut lengthwise into strips about 2 inches (5 cm) wide.

4. **Choose** a serving dish that will hold 4–5 layers of bell peppers, and line the bottom with a layer.

5. **Crumble** the anchovy fillets in a small bowl and add the garlic, parsley, capers, oregano, and oil. Drizzle a quarter of the mixture over the bell peppers. Cover with another layer of bell peppers and anchovy mixture. Repeat until all the ingredients have been used. Top with the basil.

6. **Set aside** to marinate for at least 2 hours before serving.

If you liked this recipe, you will love these ones too:

eggplant & bell pepper **salad**

228

ratatouille **tart**

256

spinach timbales

Spinach is rich in fiber and vitamin K and is a good source of many minerals, including calcium, iron, magnesium, and manganese.

Serves 6

30 minutes

15 minutes

1 hour

3

TIMBALES

12	ounces (350 g) bread, cubed
¾	cup (180 ml) milk
2½	pounds (1.25 kg) spinach
6	tablespoons (90 g) butter
½	cup (60 g) freshly grated Parmesan cheese
2	large eggs
½	cup (50 g) chopped almonds
⅛	teaspoon nutmeg
	Salt and freshly ground black pepper
2	carrots, cut in small cubes

SAUCE

1	cup (250 ml) dry white wine
1	scallion (green onion), chopped
1¼	cups (300 ml) heavy (double) cream
	Salt and freshly ground black pepper
½	teaspoon hot paprika
¼	teaspoon nutmeg

1. **To prepare the timbales,** put the bread in a medium bowl with the milk. Let stand until the milk has been absorbed, about 15 minutes.

2. **Put** the spinach in a saucepan with 1 cup (250 ml) of water and cook over medium-high heat for 3 minutes. Drain, press out excess moisture, and chop coarsely.

3. **Heat** 3 tablespoons of butter in a large frying pan over medium heat. Add the spinach and sauté for 2 minutes.

4. **Process** one-third of the spinach in a food processor with the soaked bread, Parmesan, eggs, almonds, remaining 3 tablespoons butter, and nutmeg until finely chopped. Season with salt and pepper.

5. **Preheat** the oven to 375°F (190°C/gas 5). Butter six 1-cup (250-ml) ramekins.

6. **Spoon** the chopped spinach mixture into the bottom and up the sides of the ramekins. Fill the centers with the whole spinach leaves. Add the carrots and cover with the remaining spinach.

7. **Half fill** a large roasting pan with hot water and place the ramekins in the waterbath.

8. **Bake** for 50 minutes. Remove the ramekins from the waterbath and set aside for 10 minutes. Carefully invert and turn out onto serving plates.

9. **To prepare the sauce,** bring the wine to a boil with the scallion in a small saucepan. Simmer until the wine has reduced by half. Stir in the cream and return to a boil.

10. **Season** with salt and pepper and spoon over the timbales. Dust with the paprika and nutmeg and serve hot.

easy potato knishes

A knish is an Eastern European Jewish or Yiddish baked or fried dumpling usually eaten as a snack or appetizer. This recipe is especially simple and quick.

🍲 Serves 4–6

🥘 25 minutes

🧁 55–70 minutes

6	large potatoes, peeled
6	large eggs, lightly beaten
	Salt and freshly ground white pepper
6	tablespoons potato starch

🍸 1

1. **Preheat** the oven to 350°F (180°C/gas 4). Butter a large baking sheet.

2. **Cook** the potatoes in salted, boiling water until tender, 20–25 minutes. Drain and transfer to a large bowl. Mash until smooth.

3. **Add** the eggs, beating until well blended. Season with salt and pepper.

Stir in the potato starch. The mixture should be fairly dry. Shape into balls, adding more potato starch if needed.

4. **Arrange** the knishes on the prepared baking sheet. Bake for 35–45 minutes, until golden brown. Serve warm.

If you liked this recipe, you will love these ones too:

parmesan **puffs**

74

herb **rolls**

120

pea & pecorino ring

244

pea & pecorino ring

Pecorino is an Italian cheese made from ewe's milk. If you can't find it, substitute with Parmesan in this recipe.

Serves 6–8

30 minutes

75 minutes

20 minutes

2

1½ tablespoons active dry yeast
¾ cup (180 ml) milk, hot
3⅓ cups (500 g) all-purpose (plain) flour
½ teaspoon salt
4 large eggs, lightly beaten
2 tablespoons sugar

¾ cup (180 g) butter, cut up
¼ teaspoon freshly ground black pepper
1½ cups (200 g) freshly grated pecorino cheese
1 cup (150 g) frozen peas, lightly cooked

1. Combine the yeast and milk in a small bowl. Let stand until frothy, about 15 minutes.

2. Sift the flour and salt into a large bowl. Add the yeast mixture, eggs, sugar, butter, and pepper to the flour to make a firm dough. Stir in the pecorino and peas.

3. Knead in the bowl with a dough hook or by hand on a lightly floured work

surface until smooth and elastic, 5–10 minutes.

4. Butter a 10-inch (26-cm) ring mold. Put the dough in the mold. Let rise in a warm place for about 1 hour.

5. Preheat the oven to 375°F (190°C/ gas 5). Bake for 25–35 minutes, until well risen and golden brown. Slice and serve warm or at room temperature.

If you liked this recipe, you will love these ones too:

zucchini & chive **muffins**

116

easy potato **knishes**

242

neapolitan crêpes

This recipe makes 12 crêpes, enough for 4 to 6 people. If liked, serve the crêpes with alternative fillings, such as ratatouille (see page 36). For sweet crêpes, sprinkle with sugar and lemon juice or spread with raspberry or other fruit preserves (jam).

Serves 4–6

25 minutes

1 hour

35–45 minutes

2

CRÊPES

1	cup (150 g) all-purpose (plain) flour
	Salt
2	large eggs
1	teaspoon sugar
1	cup (250 ml) milk
4	tablespoons melted butter

FILLING

2	tablespoons extra-virgin olive oil
1	small onion, thinly sliced
1	large ripe tomato, finely chopped
2	eggplant (aubergines), finely chopped
½	cup (50 g) black olives, pitted and chopped
	Salt and freshly ground black pepper
12	ounces (300 g) fresh mozzarella (preferably made from water-buffalo milk), cut into small cubes

1. **To prepare the crêpes,** sift the flour and salt into a medium bowl. Beat in the eggs and sugar. Pour in the milk gradually, followed by 2 tablespoons of butter. Beat the batter until smooth, then set aside to rest for 1 hour.

2. **Heat** a small frying pan over medium heat and brush with ½ tablespoon of the remaining butter. Add a small ladleful of batter. Spread evenly by tipping the pan so that the batter forms a thin film. Cook until lightly browned, 1–2 minutes each side. When the edges curl slightly, it is done. Repeat with the remaining batter, adding more butter as required, until all the crêpes are cooked. Stack in a pile and keep warm in a warm oven.

3. **The crêpes** can be prepared up until this step ahead of time. Store in the refrigerator, piled one on top of the other in a covered container. Reheat before filling.

4. **To prepare the filling,** heat the oil in a large frying pan over medium heat. Add the onion and sauté until softened, 3–4 minutes.

5. **Add** the tomato, eggplant, and olives. Season with salt and pepper. Simmer until the tomato has broken down and the eggplant is tender and cooked, 15–20 minutes.

6. **Spoon** the vegetable mixture and mozzarella onto the warm crêpes, covering a quarter of the surface of each one. Fold each crêpe in four and arrange on a serving dish. Serve warm.

puff pastry vegetable parcels

Serve these puff pastries as a snack anytime. They are best warm so prepare them ahead of time and bake just before serving.

Serves 4–8

30 minutes

30–35 minutes

1

2	medium carrots, cut in small cubes	1	teaspoon dried oregano
2	medium zucchini (courgettes), thinly sliced	2	tablespoons extra-virgin olive oil
1	large leek, thinly sliced	2	rolls frozen puff pastry (about 1 pound/500 g), thawed
1	medium onion, finely chopped		
1	stalk celery, finely chopped	4	ounces (125 g) Emmental or Cheddar cheese, cut in very small cubes
	Salt and freshly ground black pepper	1	large egg, beaten

1. Preheat the oven to 350°F (180°C/gas 4). Lightly oil a baking sheet. Cook the carrots in a pot of salted, boiling water for 5 minutes. Drain well.

2. Heat the oil in a large frying pan over medium heat. Add the carrots, zucchini, leek, onion, celery, salt, pepper, and oregano and sauté until softened, about 10 minutes.

3. Unroll the sheets of pastry on a lightly floured work surface. Use a sharp knife to cut into 16 rectangles measuring about 3 x 4 inches (8 x 10 cm). Divide the vegetable filling and

cheese among eight of the rectangles, placing them in the center of each piece.

4. Brush the edges of the pastry with the egg and cover with another rectangle of pastry, pressing down on the edges to seal well.

5. Use the knife to make cuts in the tops of the pastries so that steam can escape during cooking. Place the parcels on the prepared baking sheet.

6. Bake for 15–20 minutes, until golden brown. Serve hot.

If you liked this recipe, you will love these ones too:

tiropitas

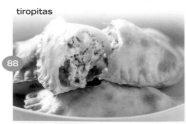

88

filled focaccia **with goat cheese**

90

spinach strudel with fruit chutney

260

zucchini flower & rice tartlets

These tartlets look very pretty with their zucchini flower decoration. Zucchini flowers are only available in the summer but you can make these tartlets at other times of the year without the flowers.

Serves 6

35 minutes

30 minutes

40–45 minutes

2

DOUGH

1 ⅓ cups (200 g) all-purpose (plain) flour

¼ teaspoon salt

6 tablespoons (90 ml) milk

3 tablespoons water

3 tablespoons extra-virgin olive oil

FILLING

4 cups (1 liter) milk

½ teaspoon salt

¾ cup (150 g) rice

2 tablespoons extra-virgin olive oil

1 shallot, chopped

4 zucchini (courgettes), thinly sliced

Salt and freshly ground black pepper

6 zucchini flowers

2 large eggs, lightly beaten

⅔ cup (80 g) freshly grated Parmesan cheese

½ teaspoon dried marjoram

¼ teaspoon freshly ground nutmeg

1 tablespoon butter, cut up

1. **To prepare the dough,** sift the flour and salt into a large bowl. Mix in the milk, water, and oil. Shape into a ball and chill in the refrigerator for 30 minutes.

2. **Preheat** the oven to 350°F (180°C/gas 4). Oil a six-cup muffin pan.

3. **To prepare the filling,** bring the milk and salt to a boil in a medium saucepan. Add the rice and cook until tender, 10–15 minutes. Remove from the heat.

4. **Heat** the oil in a large frying pan over medium heat. Add the shallot and sauté until softened, 3–4 minutes. Add the zucchini and sauté for 5 minutes. Season with salt.

5. **Blanch** the zucchini flowers in a large pot of salted, boiling water for 5 seconds. Drain.

6. **Stir** the zucchini mixture into the rice. Add the eggs, Parmesan, marjoram, and nutmeg. Season with pepper and mix well.

7. **Roll out** the dough thinly. Cut out rounds to line the muffin cups. Fill with the rice mixture and top with a zucchini flower in the center. Dot with butter.

8. **Bake** for 15–20 minutes, until golden. Serve warm or at room temperature.

asparagus & goat cheese
tartlets

You will need round, French-style goat cheese for this recipe. If you can't find it, use 1 cup (120 g) of freshly grated Fontina or Cheddar cheese. The flavor wil be different but equally good.

⦿ Serves 8

◐ 30 minutes

⦿ 30–35 minutes

♈ 2

8	ounces (250 g) asparagus stalks, coarsely chopped
2	tablespoons extra-virgin olive oil
1	clove garlic, lightly crushed but whole
	Salt and freshly ground black pepper

1	pound (500 g) frozen puff pastry, thawed
4	large eggs
1¼	cups (300 ml) milk
2	small forms semi-matured goat cheese

1. Cook the asparagus in a large pan of salted boiling water until just tender, 3–5 minutes. Drain well.

2. Heat the oil and garlic in a large frying pan over medium heat. Add the asparagus and sauté for 5 minutes. Season with salt and pepper. Discard the garlic.

3. Preheat the oven to 400°F (200°C/gas 6). Butter eight 4-inch (10-cm) tartlet pans. Line the bottom and sides with the pastry.

4. Spoon the asparagus mixture evenly into the pastry bases. Beat the eggs and milk in a medium bowl until frothy. Season with salt and pepper. Pour the mixture over the asparagus.

5. Cut the goat cheeses horizontally to make 8 rounds. Place a cheese round in each tartlet. Season with pepper. Bake for 20 minutes, until the pastry is golden and the filling is set.

6. Serve warm or at room temperature.

If you liked this recipe, you will love these ones too:

zucchini flower & rice **tartlets**

250

leek & almond quiche

254

ratatouille tart

256

leek & almond quiche

The pastry in this recipe is a good short crust that can be used for a range of quiches and savory tarts. Be sure not to overbeat in the food processor and to chill for at least an hour.

Serves 6–8

35 minutes

1 hour

35–45 minutes

2

SHORT CRUST PASTRY

2	cups (300 g) all-purpose (plain) flour
½	teaspoon salt
½	cup (125 g) butter, cut up
2–4	tablespoons ice water
2	large egg yolks

FILLING

3	large eggs
½	cup (125 ml) heavy (double) cream
½	cup (125 ml) milk
	Salt
⅔	cup (60 g) chopped almonds
⅔	cup (80 g) freshly grated Parmesan cheese
3	leeks, thinly sliced

1. To prepare the pastry, sift the flour and salt into the bowl of a food processor and pulse a few to times to add air. Add the butter and pulse briefly to cut into the flour. Add the water and egg yolks and pulse rapidly until the mixture is just crumbly.

2. Gather the crumbs and shape into a ball. Wrap in plastic wrap (cling film) and chill in the refrigerator for 1 hour.

3. Preheat the oven to 400°F (200°C/gas 6). Oil a 9-inch (23-cm) pie dish.

4. Roll out the dough into a 12-inch (30-cm) disk on a lightly floured work surface. Place the dough in the prepared dish.

5. To prepare the filling, beat the eggs, cream, milk, and salt in a medium bowl.

6. Sprinkle the pastry with the almonds and Parmesan. Top with the leeks and pour the egg mixture over the top.

7. Bake for 35–45 minutes, until golden. Serve hot or at room temperature.

If you liked this recipe, you will love these ones too:

zucchini flower & rice **tartlets**

250

asparagus & goat cheese **tartlets**

252

ratatouille tart

256

ratatouille tart

Fresh ratatouille makes a delicious filling for this tart. You could also use a mix of any of your favorite vegetables.

Serves 4–6

15 minutes

1 hour

30–40 minutes

1

2 large eggplants (aubergines), cut in small cubes
Coarse sea salt
1 pound (500 g) frozen puff pastry, thawed
¼ cup (60 ml) extra-virgin olive oil
2 medium onions, chopped
2 cloves garlic, finely chopped
3 zucchini (courgettes), sliced
3 green bell peppers, (capsicums) seeded and sliced

1 pound (500 g) tomatoes, peeled and chopped
1 bay leaf
1 tablespoon fresh thyme
Freshly ground black pepper
4 ounces (125 g) fresh mozzarella, cut into small cubes
Fresh basil leaves, to garnish

1. Sprinkle the eggplant with coarse sea salt and let drain for 1 hour.

2. Preheat the oven to 350°F (180°C/ gas 4). Grease a 10-inch (25-cm) quiche or springform pan.

3. Roll out the pastry on a lightly floured work surface to ¼ inch (5 mm) thick. Line the pan with the pastry. Bake until risen and golden brown, about 15 minutes.

4. Heat the oil in a large frying pan oven medium heat. Shake the salt off the

eggplant and add to the pan with the onions, garlic, zucchini, and bell peppers. Sauté until softened, 7–10 minutes.

5. Add the tomatoes, bay leaf, and thyme. Mix well and simmer until the vegetables are tender, 10–15 minutes. Season with pepper.

6. Spoon the ratatouille into the pastry case. Top with mozzarella and place under a broiler (grill) for 5 minutes, until just melted. Sprinkle with the basil and serve hot.

If you liked this recipe, you will love these ones too:

crostini **with ratatouille**

36

leek & almond quiche

254

tomato & pesto puff

262

vegetarian strudel

If preferred, make this strudel using eight sheets of phyllo pastry instead of the short crust pastry. Brush each sheet with melted butter and lay one over the other. Cover with the filling and roll up and bake following the instructions below.

Serves 4–6

35 minutes

1 hour

40-45 minutes

2

1	quantity Short Crust Pastry (see page 254)
4	tablespoons (60 ml) extra-virgin olive oil
1	clove garlic, chopped
1/3	cup (60 g) pine nuts
1	pound (500 g) zucchini (courgettes), grated
	Salt

1	pound (500 g) fresh ricotta cheese
2/3	cup (80 g) freshly grated Parmesan cheese
1	large egg + 1 large egg yolk
6–8	leaves basil, torn
	Salad greens and cherry tomatoes to serve (optional)

1. **Prepare** the pastry and chill in the refrigerator.

2. **Preheat** the oven to 350°F (180°C/gas 4). Line a baking sheet with parchment paper.

3. **Heat** 3 tablespoons of oil in a large frying pan over medium heat. Add the garlic and pine nuts and sauté until pale gold, 3–5 minutes.

4. **Add** the zucchini and sauté until almost tender, about 5 minutes. Season with salt.

5. **Mix** the ricotta, Parmesan, egg, egg yolk, basil, and salt in a large bowl.

6. **Roll** the pastry out very thinly on a lightly floured work surface into a large rectangle.

7. **Spread** with the ricotta mixture, leaving a 3/4 inch (2 cm) border around the edges. Arrange the zucchini mixture on top. Fold in the edges down the long side, then roll the pastry up from the short sides over the filling.

8. **Transfer** to the prepared baking sheet. Brush with the remaining 1 tablespoon of oil and bake for 30–35 minutes, until golden brown. Serve hot with salad greens and cherry tomatoes, if liked.

If you liked this recipe, you will love these ones too:

asparagus & goat cheese tartlets

252

spinach strudel with fruit chutney

260

tomato & pesto puff

262

spinach strudel
with fruit chutney

Spinach is full of health-giving properties but should always be eaten as fresh as possible. Don't buy wilted spinach as most of the nutrients will be gone. Frozen spinach is flash frozen and retains a lot of its natural goodness.

- Serves 6
- 30 minutes
- 10 minutes
- 35 minutes

Y 2

1	pound (500 g) spinach
4	tablespoons (60 g) butter
1	clove garlic, finely chopped
	Salt
1	pound (500 g) frozen puff pastry, thawed

5	ounces (150 g) Emmental cheese, thinly sliced
1¼	cups (300 g) fruit chutney
1	large egg, lightly beaten

1. **Preheat** the oven to 400°F (200°C/ gas 6). Butter a large baking sheet.

2. **Cook** the spinach in 1 cup (250 ml) of water for 2–3 minutes. Drain and set aside to cool a little, about 10 minutes.

3. **Chop** the spinach finely, squeezing out any excess moisture. Heat 3 tablespoons of butter in a large frying pan over medium. Add the garlic and spinach and sauté for 5 minutes. Season with salt.

4. **Roll** the pastry out very thinly in a large rectangle on a lightly floured work surface. Cover with the spinach, Emmental, and chutney. Tuck the short ends in and carefully roll the pastry and filling into a strudel.

5. **Transfer** to the prepared baking sheet and make several cuts in the top. Brush with the beaten egg.

6. **Bake** for 30–35 minutes, until golden brown. Serve hot.

If you liked this recipe, you will love these ones too:

spinach **timbales**

240

vegetarian **strudel**

258

tomato & pesto puff

This recipe is quick and easy to prepare and makes a healthy snack for hungry school children.

Serves 4

15 minutes

15–20 minutes

1	pound (500 g) ripe tomatoes
1	cup (50 g) fresh basil
1/3	cup (90 ml) extra-virgin olive oil

8	ounces (250 g) frozen puff pastry, thawed
	Salt and freshly ground black pepper

1

1. **Preheat** the oven to 350°F (180°C/ gas 4.

2. **Cut** the tomatoes in half and squeeze out the juice and seeds. Use a sharp knife to slice the tomatoes thinly then lay them on paper towels to absorb any excess liquid. Turn over to drain the other side on a clean paper towel.

3. **Reserve** 4–6 leaves of basil to garnish. Process the remaining basil with the oil in a food processor to make a smooth pesto.

4. **Roll** the dough out into a large circle or rectangle about $1/8$ inch (3 mm) thick. Brush with the pesto. Place the tomatoes on top of the pastry and brush again with the pesto. Season with salt and pepper.

5. **Bake** for 15–20 minutes, until the pastry is risen and golden brown. Garnish with the reserved basil leaves and serve hot.

If you liked this recipe, you will love these ones too:

baby focaccias **with tomato & prosciutto**
92

cheese & tomato **pinwheels**
114

quick cheese & onion bread
130

herb tempura

Tempura is a Japanese dish consisting of deep-fried vegetables, fish, or meat. In this recipe we have used a typical light tempura batter to coat fresh herbs before frying them quickly in oil. Always serve hot, straight from the pan.

Serves 10–12

45 minutes

15 minutes

2

- ⅔ cup (100 g) all-purpose (plain) flour
- ⅓ cup (90 ml) sparkling mineral water
- 1 cup (250 ml) sunflower oil, for frying

- 24 sage leaves
- 24 wild garlic leaves
- 16 sprigs fresh parsley
- 12 large basil leaves
     Salt

1. **Place** the flour in a large bowl and add the water. Beat with a whisk to make a smooth batter.

2. **Heat** the oil in a large frying pan over medium heat. Test the oil temperature by dropping in a small piece of bread. If it immediately bubbles to the surface and begins to turn golden, the oil is ready.

3. **Dip** the herbs in the batter and then drop them in the oil. Fry until golden brown, 2–3 minutes.

4. **Scoop out** with a slotted spoon and drain on paper towels. Sprinkle with salt and serve hot.

If you liked this recipe, you will love these ones too:

fresh sage leaf **fritters**

266

deep fried **okra**

268

sicilian eggplant fritters

276

fresh sage leaf fritters

In ancient times sage was known as a wonder herb and used to cure many different health problems. It is now believed to help improve mood and aid digestion.

Serves 4

10 minutes

5–10 minutes

2

2   cups (500 ml) oil, for frying
40   large leaves fresh sage
½   cup (75 g) all-purpose (plain) flour
1   large egg, beaten until foamy with a pinch of salt

1⅓   cups (200 g) fine dry bread crumbs
Salt

1. **Heat** the oil in a large frying pan until very hot. Test the oil temperature by dropping in a small piece of bread. If it immediately bubbles to the surface and begins to turn golden, the oil is ready.

2. **Rinse** the sage leaves under cold running water. Shake off the excess water and dredge the damp leaves in the flour. Dip in the egg, then coat well in the bread crumbs.

3. **Add** half the sage leaves to the oil; they will turn golden brown almost immediately. Turn them once, then scoop out with a slotted spoon. Drain on paper towels. Cook the remaining leaves in the same way.

4. **Sprinkle** with salt and serve hot.

If you liked this recipe, you will love these ones too:

meatballs with sage butter

216

herb tempura

264

deep fried okra

Originally from Africa, okra is popular in the southern United States. It is a very good source of dietary fiber and of many vitamins and minerals.

- Serves 4
- 10 minutes
- 1 hour
- 10–15 minutes

- 1

1	large egg
1	cup (150 g) all-purpose (plain) flour
1	cup (250 ml) iced water
4	cups (1 liter) live oil, for frying
1	pound (500 g) fresh okra

1. **Beat** the egg in a large bowl until frothy. Whisk in the flour and water to make a batter. Let rest for 1 hour.

2. **Heat** the oil in a large frying pan until very hot. Test the oil temperature by dropping in a small piece of bread. If it immediately bubbles to the surface and begins to turn golden, the oil is ready.

3. **Dip** the okra in the batter. Fry in small batches until crisp and golden brown, about 5 minutes. Drain on paper towels and serve hot.

If you liked this recipe, you will love these ones too:

herb tempura

264

fresh sage leaf fritters

266

zucchini fritters with tzatziki dip

270

zucchini fritters with tzatziki dip

Serve these tasty fritters straight from the pan.

Serves 6–8

20 minutes

10–15 minutes

1

FRITTERS

1½	pounds (750 g) zucchini (courgettes), grated
1	large white onion, grated
½	cup (75 g) all-purpose (plain) flour
3	large eggs, lightly beaten
1	tablespoon finely chopped fresh mint
1	tablespoon finely chopped fresh parsley
	Salt and freshly ground black pepper
½	cup (125 ml) extra-virgin olive oil

TZATZIKI

1	cup (250 g) plain Greek-style yogurt
1	small cucumber, grated
1	clove garlic, finely chopped
1	tablespoon finely chopped fresh mint
1	tablespoon freshly squeezed lemon juice

1. **To prepare the fritters,** squeeze the excess moisture out of the grated zucchini. Combine the zucchini, onion, flour, eggs, mint, and parsley in a large bowl. Season with salt and pepper and mix well.

2. **Heat** the oil in a large frying pan until very hot. Test the oil temperature by dropping in a small piece of bread. If it immediately bubbles to the surface and begins to turn golden, the oil is ready.

3. **Add** heaped tablespoons of the zucchini batter to the oil and flatten slightly. Fry until golden brown on one side, 3–4 minutes. Turn and fry until the other side is golden brown. Drain on paper towels.

4. **To prepare the tzatziki dip,** combine the yogurt, cucumber, garlic, mint, and lemon juice in a small bowl.

5. **Serve** the fritters hot with the tzatziki dip passed separately.

If you liked this recipe, you will love these ones too:

deep fried **okra**

268

onion bhajis **with yogurt dip**

272

onion fritters **with balsamic vinegar**

274

onion bhajis with yogurt dip

For a change use ladyfinger (okra), cauliflower, or thinly sliced potatoes instead of scallions (spring onions).

○ Serves 6

20–25 minutes

1 hour

15–20 minutes

2

YOGURT DIP

¼	cup (50 g) fresh creamy goat cheese
2	tablespoons milk
1	cup (250 ml) plain low-fat yogurt
½	teaspoon salt
1	tablespoon finely chopped fresh mint leaves
¼	teaspoon freshly ground black pepper
¼	teaspoon garam masala
¼	teaspoon paprika

BHAJIS

1	cup (150 g) gram (chickpea) flour
2	tablespoons all-purpose (plain) flour
½	teaspoon ground cumin
1	teaspoon ground coriander
1½	teaspoons fine sea salt
	Pinch of cayenne pepper
½–⅔	cup (120–150 ml) water
1	teaspoon black mustard seeds, toasted
1	teaspoon fennel seeds, toasted
8	ounces (250 g) scallions (spring onions), thickly sliced
3	long green chiles (about 2 inches/5 cm), seeded and finely chopped
2	tablespoons finely chopped fresh cilantro (coriander)
4	cups (1 liter) vegetable oil, for frying

1. **To prepare the dip,** mash the cheese with the milk in a medium bowl. Beat in the yogurt until smooth. Mix in the salt and mint. Sprinkle the pepper, garam masala, and paprika in a pattern on top of the yogurt. Don't stir them in. Chill in the refrigerator until needed.

2. **To prepare the bhajis,** combine both flours and the ground spices in a large bowl. Add the salt and cayenne and gradually whisk in sufficient water until you have a smooth paste-like batter. Stir in the toasted seeds, scallions, chiles and cilantro. Gradually whisk in enough of the remaining water to make a thick batter.

3. **Heat** the oil in a deep-fryer or deep saucepan until very hot. Test the oil temperature by dropping in a small piece of bread. If it immediately bubbles to the surface and begins to turn golden, the oil is ready.

4. **Add** a few spoonfuls of the mixture to the oil and fry until crisp and golden, about 5 minutes. Remove with a slotted spoon and drain on paper towels. Repeat until all the mixture is cooked.

5. **Arrange** the bhajis on a dish and serve hot with the yogurt dip.

onion fritters
with balsamic vinegar

Balsamic vinegar originally comes from the city of Modena, in central Italy, where it has been made for over a thousand years.

Serves 4–6

15 minutes

30 minutes

20 minutes

1

4	tablespoons (60 ml) extra-virgin olive oil
4	large onions, thinly sliced
4	large eggs
	Salt
½	cup (60 g) freshly grated Parmesan cheese

½	cup (75 g) fine dry bread crumbs
1	cup (250 ml) oil, for frying
	Balsamic vinegar, to taste

1. **Heat** the extra-virgin oil in a large frying pan over medium heat. Add the onions and sauté until lightly browned, about 5 minutes.

2. **Beat** the eggs with a pinch of salt in a bowl, then stir in the Parmesan and bread crumbs.

3. **Add** the onions and mix well. Set aside for at least 30 minutes.

4. **Heat** the oil to very hot in a large frying pan. Test the oil temperature by dropping in a small piece of bread. If it immediately bubbles to the surface and begins to turn golden, the oil is ready.

5. **Drop** spoonfuls of the onion mixture into the oil and fry until golden brown, about 5 minutes each batch. Scoop out with a slotted spoon and drain on paper towels.

6. **Drizzle** with balsamic vinegar and serve hot.

If you liked this recipe, you will love these ones too:

onion bhajis **with yogurt dip**

272

sicilian **eggplant fritters**

276

sicilian eggplant fritters

Eggplant, also known as aubergine, is a healthy food choice. It is rich in copper, folate, magnesium, and potassium and provides plenty of dietary fiber.

Serves 4–6

20 minutes

40–50 minutes

2

2	eggplants (aubergines)
2	tablespoons finely chopped fresh parsley
2	tablespoons finely chopped fresh basil
1	clove garlic, finely chopped
¼	cup (30 g) freshly grated Parmesan cheese

2	large eggs, lightly beaten
	Salt and freshly ground black pepper
1	cup (150 g) fine dry bread crumbs
1	cup (250 ml) olive oil, for frying

1. **Preheat** the oven to 400°F (200°C/ gas 6). Cut the eggplants in half lengthwise and place them on a baking sheet. Bake for 20–30 minutes, until tender and golden brown. Let cool a little then scoop out the flesh with a spoon. Mash coarsely with a fork.

2. **Stir together** the eggplant, parsley, basil, garlic, cheese, eggs, salt, pepper, and enough bread crumbs to make a firm mixture. Shape into balls the size of walnuts. Roll in the remaining bread crumbs.

3. **Heat** the oil in a large frying pan until very hot. Test the oil temperature by dropping in a small piece of bread. If it immediately bubbles to the surface and begins to turn golden, the oil is ready.

4. **Fry** the fritters in batches until golden brown all over, 5–7 minutes each batch. Drain on paper towels and serve hot.

If you liked this recipe, you will love these ones too:

zucchini fritters **with tzatziki dip**

270

onion bhajis **with yogurt dip**

272

onion fritters **with balsamic vinegar**

274

fried parmesan puffs

Serve a bowl of these wickedly good little cheese puffs with pre-dinner drinks.

Serves 6

15 minutes

20 minutes

1	cup (250 ml) water
1	teaspoon salt
3	tablespoons butter
1	cup (150 g) all-purpose (plain) flour
4	large eggs

1	cup (120 g) freshly grated Parmesan cheese
1/2	cup (60 g) freshly grated Emmenthal cheese
	Dash of nutmeg
2	cups (500 ml) oil, for frying

2

1. Combine the water with the salt and butter in a saucepan over medium heat and bring to a boil.

2. Add the flour all at once, remove from heat, and stir vigorously with a wooden spoon until the mixture is smooth. Return to low heat and simmer until the batter pulls away from the sides of the pan. Let cool a little.

3. Add the eggs one at a time mixing each one in before adding the next.

4. Add both cheeses and the nutmeg. Mold the mixture into marble-size balls.

5. Heat the oil in a deep-fryer or deep saucepan until very hot. Test the oil temperature by dropping in a small piece of bread. If it immediately bubbles to the surface and begins to turn golden, the oil is ready.

6. Fry the puffs in small batches until crisp and golden brown, about 5 minutes each batch. Drain on paper towels and serve hot.

If you liked this recipe, you will love these ones too:

parmesan **puffs**

74

croquettes **with ham & cheese**

198

fried mozzarella

280

fried mozzarella

You will need high quality fresh mozzarella cheese for this dish.

- Serves 4
- 10 minutes
- 10–15 minutes

½ cup (75 g) all-purpose (plain) flour

2 large eggs

1⅓ cups (200 g) fine dry bread crumbs

8 ounces (250 g) fresh mozzarella cheese, thickly sliced

2 cups (500 ml) oil, for frying
Salt

1

1. Place the flour in one shallow bowl, the eggs in another, and the bread crumbs in a third.

2. Dredge the mozzarella in the flour, shaking off any excess. Dip in the beaten eggs and then in the bread crumbs.

3. Heat the oil in a deep-fryer or deep saucepan until very hot. Test the oil temperature by dropping in a small piece of bread. If it immediately bubbles to the surface and begins to turn golden, the oil is ready.

4. Fry the mozzarella in batches until golden brown on both sides, about 5 minutes each batch. Drain on paper towels, sprinkle with salt, and serve hot.

If you liked this recipe, you will love these ones too:

fried polenta **with mushrooms, peas & cheese**

56

croquettes **with ham & cheese**

198

fried parmesan puffs

278

Something
Sweet

strawberry & champagne granita

Serve this delicious granita in tiny chilled dessert glasses. If liked, use a very dry Italian Prosecco instead of the Champagne.

Serves 8–12

20 minutes

4–5 hours

2

3 cups (450 g) fresh strawberries, sliced

2 cups (300 g) confectioners' (icing) sugar

1 (750 ml) bottle chilled dry Champagne

Fresh mint leaves, to serve

1. **Reserve** a few slices of strawberry to garnish. Combine the remaining strawberries in a bowl with the confectioners' sugar. Let rest in the refrigerator for 1 hour.

2. **Purée** the strawberry mixture in a food processor or blender until smooth. Stir in the Champagne.

3. **Place** in a freezerproof bowl and freeze for 1 hour. Use a fork or hand blender to break the granita up into large crystals.

4. **If using an ice cream machine,** transfer to the machine at this point and follow the manufacturers' instructions for granita.

5. **To continue by hand,** replace the bowl in the freezer for 30 minutes, then break up again with a fork. Repeat 3–5 times, until the crystals are frozen.

6. **Scoop** the granita into 8–12 small dessert glasses. Garnish with the reserved slices of strawberry and the mint leaves and serve.

If you liked this recipe, you will love these ones too:

tomato **sorbet**

222

kiwi **sorbet**

286

melon **sorbet** with orange & basil

288

kiwi sorbet

Kiwis contain more vitamin C than any other fruit. They also contain useful amounts of dietary fiber, potassium, and vitamin E.

- ◉ Serves 8–12
- ◖ 20 minutes
- ◗ 30 minutes
- ◍ 2–3 minutes

🍴 2

1	cup (200 g) sugar
1¼	cups (300 ml) water
6	ripe kiwi fruit, peeled
1	tablespoon Cointreau
	Slices of mandarin, to garnish

1. **Place** the sugar and ³/4 cup (200 ml) of water in a medium saucepan over medium heat and bring to a boil. Simmer until the sugar has completely dissolved, 2–3 minutes. Remove from the heat and let cool, about 30 minutes.

2. **Chop** the kiwi fruit in a food processor until smooth. Press through a fine-mesh strainer to remove the seeds.

3. **Weigh out** ³/4 cup (200 ml) of the purée and stir it into the sugar syrup. Stir in the Cointreau and remaining ¹/2 cup (125 ml) water.

4. **Transfer** to your ice cream machine and freeze following the manufacturer's instructions.

5. **Serve** in 8–12 small dessert glasses. Garnish with the mandarin, if desired.

If you liked this recipe, you will love these ones too:

strawberry & champagne granita

284

melon sorbet with orange & basil

288

melon sorbet
with orange & basil

This sorbet is so easy to make and a joy to serve. Because everything depends on the taste of the melon, be sure to choose only the most fragrant fruit available.

- Serves 8–12
- 15 minutes
- About 2 hours

1   pound (500 g) cantaloupe (rock) melon flesh, peeled weight, cut in cubes

6   fresh basil leaves + extra to garnish

$\frac{1}{3}$ cup (90 ml) freshly squeezed orange juice

$\frac{3}{4}$ cup (150 g) superfine (caster) sugar

$\frac{1}{4}$ teaspoon salt

1

1. **Place** the melon cubes and basil in a blender with the orange juice, sugar, and salt. Chop until the sugar has dissolved and the mixture is smooth, about 30 seconds.

2. **Transfer** to a bowl and chill in the refrigerator for 1 hour.

3. **Transfer** to your ice cream machine and freeze following the manufacturer's instructions.

4. **Pipe** the frozen sorbet into 8–12 small dessert glasses. Garnish with the extra basil leaves and serve.

If you liked this recipe, you will love these ones too:

tomato **sorbet**

222

strawberry & champagne **granita**

284

kiwi sorbet

286

chocolate spumone
with pistachios

A spumone is an Italian dessert made with melted chocolate or sweetened puréed fruit which is folded into whipped cream. Spumones are simple to make and delicious to eat.

Serves 8

15 minutes

About 1 hour

1

4	ounces (125 g) dark chocolate, chopped
¾	cup (200 ml) boiling water
2	cups (500 ml) heavy (double) cream
1	cup (200 g) superfine (caster) sugar

1	teaspoon vanilla extract (essence)
⅛	teaspoon salt
	Dark chocolate curls, to serve
	Coarsely chopped pistachios, to serve

1. **Place** eight small (⅔ cup/150 ml) glasses in the freezer to chill.

2. **Put** the chocolate in a medium bowl and pour in the boiling water. Stir until the chocolate has melted completely. Let cool then chill in the refrigerator for 30 minutes.

3. **Beat** the cream in a large bowl with an electric mixer on high speed until thick. Fold the cream into the chilled chocolate mixture. Stir in the sugar, vanilla, and salt.

4. **Transfer** the mixture to your ice cream machine and freeze following the manufacturer's instructions until creamy and almost frozen, 20–25 minutes.

5. **Pipe** the spumone into the chilled glasses. Garnish with the chocolate curls and pistachios and serve.

If you liked this recipe, you will love these ones too:

chocolate hedgehogs

296

chocolate truffles

308

chocolate walnut fudge

312

mini margarita muffins

Serve these tiny muffins with a cup of tea or coffee for morning or afternoon tea. They are also good at breakfast and brunch.

Serves 12

20 minutes

30 minutes

20 minutes

1

½ cup (60 g) golden raisins (sultanas)

2 tablespoons tequila

2 tablespoons freshly squeezed lime juice

2 cups (300 g) all-purpose (plain) flour

½ cup (100 g) sugar

1 teaspoon baking powder

1 teaspoon baking soda (bicarbonate of soda)

2 large eggs, lightly beaten

1 cup (250 ml) milk

1 tablespoon finely grated lemon zest

1 tablespoon finely grated lime zest

Salt

1. **Soak** the raisins in the tequila and lime juice for 30 minutes.

2. **Preheat** the oven to 400°F (200°C/gas 6). Lightly oil two 24-cup mini muffins tins.

3. **Combine** the flour, sugar, baking powder, and baking soda in a large bowl.

4. **Make** a well in the center and pour in the eggs and milk. Stir in the lemon and lime zest together with the golden raisins and their soaking liquid. Mix until smooth.

5. **Spoon** the batter into the prepared muffin tins and sprinkle lightly with salt. Bake until risen and golden brown, about 20 minutes.

6. **Let cool** in the muffin tins for 5 minutes then turn our onto a wire rack. Serve warm or at room temperature.

If you liked this recipe, you will love these ones too:

chocolate macadamia **cupcakes**

294

raspberry **tartlets**

298

lemon tartlets

300

chocolate macadamia
cupcakes

These cupcakes are quick and easy to prepare. They don't contain egg so can be served to people with egg allergies.

Serves 18

20 minutes

25–30 minutes

1

CUPCAKES

2	cups (300 g) all-purpose (plain) flour
4	tablespoons unsweetened cocoa powder, sifted
1	teaspoon ground cinnamon
1/4	teaspoon ground cloves
1/8	teaspoon salt
1	cup (250 g) unsalted butter
1	cup (200 g) firmly packed light brown sugar
1/2	teaspoon baking soda (bicarbonate of soda)
1/2	tablespoon warm water
1	cup (250 ml) milk
1/2	cup (90 g) macadamia nuts, coarsely chopped
1/2	cup (90 g) milk chocolate chips

TOPPING

1 1/2	cups (225 g) confectioners' (icing) sugar
2	tablespoons unsweetened cocoa powder, sifted
2	tablespoons water
1/2	teaspoon vanilla extract (essence)
1/3	cup (50 g) macadamia nuts, coarsely chopped and lightly toasted

1. **Preheat** the oven to 325°F (170°C/gas 3). Line two standard 12-cup muffin tins with 18 paper liners.

2. **To prepare the cupcakes,** combine the flour, cocoa, cinnamon, cloves, and salt in a small bowl.

3. **Beat** the butter and brown sugar in a medium bowl with an electric mixer on medium-high speed until creamy.

4. **Dissolve** the baking soda in the water and add to the butter mixture. With mixer on low speed, add the mixed dry ingredients and milk. Stir the macadamias and chocolate chips in by hand.

5. **Spoon** the batter into the prepared muffin tins, filling each cup three-quarters full.

6. **Bake** for 25–30 minutes, until risen and firm to the touch. Transfer the muffin tins to a wire rack. Let cool completely before removing the cupcakes.

7. **To prepare the topping,** combine the confectioners' sugar, cocoa, water, and vanilla in a small bowl, stirring until smooth.

8. **Spread** the frosting over the cupcakes and top with the macadamia nuts.

chocolate hedgehogs

Prepare these miniature hedgehogs for a children's birthday party.

Serves 12

40 minutes

30 minutes

5 minutes

2

4 ounces (125 g) milk chocolate, coarsely chopped

4 ounces (125 g) dark chocolate, coarsely chopped

1 tablespoon sugar

1 tablespoon water

²/₃ cup (150 ml) heavy (double) cream

1 cup (125 g) plain (or vanilla) cookie crumbs

2 teaspoon vanilla extract (essence)

¹/₃ cup (50 g) unsweetened cocoa powder

¹/₂ cup (90 g) pine nuts

1 tablespoon candied (glacé) cherries

1. **Combine** both types of chocolate with the sugar, water, and cream in a medium saucepan over low heat and stir until the chocolate has melted.

2. **Remove** from the heat and stir in the cookie crumbs and vanilla. Refrigerate for 30 minutes until firm.

3. **Shape** into oblongs about the size of walnuts and dust with the cocoa. Stick the pine nuts in the top to make them look like hedgehogs.

4. **Cut up** the cherries and use them to form eyes. Chill in the refrigerator until ready to serve.

If you liked this recipe, you will love these ones too:

chocolate macadamia **cupcakes**

294

chocolate **truffles**

308

chocolate walnut **fudge**

312

raspberry tartlets

These scrumptious little tarts can be prepared in just a few minutes. Replace the raspberries with other types of fresh fruit, such as sliced strawberries or bananas, or whole blueberries.

Serves 6–12

20 minutes

30 minutes

12–15 minutes

1

8	ounces (250 g) frozen puff pastry, thawed	1	tablespoon confectioners' (icing) sugar
1	cup (250 ml) heavy (double) cream	1 1/2	cups (250 g) fresh raspberries

1. **Preheat** the oven to 400°F (200°C/ gas 6). Rinse twelve 2-inch (5-cm) tartlet pans with cold water.

2. **Roll** the pastry to 1/8 inch (3 mm) thick on a lightly floured work surface. Use a pastry cutter to cut out rounds to fit the tartlet pans and line the pans. Prick the pastry with a fork.

3. **Bake** for 12–15 minutes, until the pastry is golden brown. Let cool on a wire rack, at least 30 minutes.

4. **Beat** the cream and confectioners' sugar in a medium bowl until thick. Spoon into a pastry bag and pipe into the tarts. Place the raspberries on top and serve.

If you liked this recipe, you will love these ones too:

lemon **tartlets**

300

pecan **tartlets**

302

frosted mini almond palmiers

304

lemon tartlets

Replace the lemon with lime for a slightly different but equally delicious citrus flavor. If short of time, use 1 cup (250 g) of store-bought lemon curd to fill the tartlets.

Serves 12

30 minutes

1 hour

12–15 minutes

2

LEMON CURD

⅓ cup (70 g) superfine (caster) sugar

¼ cup (60 ml) freshly squeezed lemon juice

2 teaspoons finely grated lemon zest

3 large egg yolks

¼ cup (60 g) unsalted butter, cubed

TARTLETS

2 cups (300 g) all-purpose (plain) flour

⅛ teaspoon salt

½ cup (125 g) butter, softened

½ cup (100 g) sugar

1 large egg yolk

Finely grated zest of 1 lemon

½ teaspoon lemon extract (essence)

1. **To prepare the lemon curd,** stir the sugar, lemon juice, and zest in a small saucepan over medium heat until the sugar dissolves.

2. **Whisk** the egg yolks in a heatproof bowl and gradually add the hot lemon mixture. Strain the mixture through a fine-mesh sieve. Return to the heatproof bowl and place over a saucepan of barely simmering water. Cook, stirring continuously, until the mixture coats the back of a wooden spoon. Do not allow the mixture to boil.

3. **Remove** from the heat and add the butter cubes, one at a time, stirring until fully combined. Refrigerate for 1 hour, until cooled.

4. **To prepare the tartlets,** sift the flour and salt into a bowl. Beat the butter and sugar in a large bowl with an electric mixer until creamy.

5. **Add** the egg yolk, lemon zest, and lemon extract, beating until just blended. Mix in the dry ingredients. Cover with plastic wrap (cling film) and refrigerate for 30 minutes.

6. **Preheat** the oven to 350°F (180°C/ gas 4). Set out two 12-cup mini muffin pans. Form the dough into balls the size of walnuts and press into the cups. Prick well with a fork.

7. **Bake** for 12–15 minutes, until just golden. Transfer to racks to cool. Fill with a teaspoon of lemon curd.

If you liked this recipe, you will love these ones too:

raspberry **tartlets**

298

pecan **tartlets**

302

frosted mini almond palmiers

304

pecan tartlets

Pecans are an American nut, and their name comes from a Native American word to describe nuts that need a stone to be cracked. Packed with protein, vitamin E, thiamine, and many other nutrients, pecans are a healthy food choice.

Serves 12–15

30 minutes

30 minutes

12–15 minutes

2

TARTLETS

½	cup (120 g) cream cheese, softened
½	cup (125 g) butter, softened
1	cup (150 g) all-purpose (plain) flour

FILLING

2	large eggs
½	cup (100 g) firmly packed dark brown sugar
2	tablespoons butter, melted
½	teaspoon vanilla extract (essence)
⅛	teaspoon salt
1	cup (150 g) coarsely chopped pecans

1. **Preheat** the oven to 350°F (180°C/gas 4). Butter twenty-four mini muffin cups.

2. **To prepare the tartlets,** beat the cream cheese and butter in a large bowl with an electric mixer at high speed until creamy. Mix in the flour to form a smooth dough.

3. **Roll out** the dough on a lightly floured surface to a thickness of $^1/8$ inch (3 mm) inch. Use a 2-inch (5-cm) fluted cookie cutter to cut out 24 dough rounds. Press the dough rounds into the prepared muffin cups.

4. **To prepare the filling,** beat the eggs in a large bowl until frothy. Beat in the brown sugar, butter, vanilla, and salt. Stir in the pecans. Spoon the filling into the cups.

5. **Bake** for 15–20 minutes, until golden and a toothpick inserted into the center comes out clean. Transfer to racks and let cool completely before serving.

If you liked this recipe, you will love these ones too:

raspberry **tartlets**

298

lemon **tartlets**

300

frosted mini almond palmiers

304

frosted mini almond palmiers

The tasty little pastries can be served with or without the frosting.

Serves 12–15

30 minutes

30 minutes

10–12 minutes

2

PALMIERS

2	sheets frozen puff pastry (about 1 pound/500 g), thawed
½	cup (100 g) superfine (caster) sugar
2	tablespoons slivered almonds

FROSTING

2	cups (300 g) confectioners (icing) sugar
2	tablespoons butter
1	teaspoon vanilla extract (essence)
2	tablespoons boiling water

1. **Preheat** the oven to 400°F (200°C/gas 6). Butter two cookie sheets.

2. **To prepare the palmiers,** sprinkle 3–4 tablespoons of sugar on a work surface. Unfold or unroll the pastry on the sugar and make four equal-size rectangles. Sprinkle the top of each piece with 2–3 tablespoons of sugar. Roll the long sides of each rectangle to meet in the center.

3. **Cut** the pastry rolls crosswise into ½-inch (1-cm) thick slices. Place the cookies 2 inches (5 cm) apart on the prepared cookie sheets. Sprinkle with the remaining sugar and the almonds.

4. **Bake** for 10–12 minutes, until just golden on the bottom. Remove from the oven and turn the pastries over. Bake for 5–7 minutes more, or until golden. Transfer to racks and let cool completely.

5. **To prepare the frosting,** combine the confectioners' sugar, butter, and vanilla extract in a bowl. Add enough of the boiling water to make a creamy frosting.

6. **Drizzle** the frosting over the palmiers. Let set before serving.

If you liked this recipe, you will love these ones too:

lemon **tartlets**

300

pecan **tartlets**

302

petits-fours

A petit-four is a tiny fancy cake, cookie, or sweet, typically made with marzipan and beautifully frosted. The name, which means "little oven" in French, probably comes from the small ovens that were used for baking such confections in the 18th century. It is best to make petits fours one or two days in advance.

🍴 Serves 12–15

⏱ 1 hour

🌡 5 hours

⏲ 15–20 minutes

🍸 3

PETITS-FOURS

- ⅔ cup (100 g) all-purpose (plain) flour
- ⅛ teaspoon salt
- 4 large eggs
- ½ cup (100 g) superfine (caster) sugar
- ¼ cup (60 g) butter, melted
- ⅓ cup (100 g) apricot preserves (jam), warmed
- 8 ounces (250 g) marzipan, softened

FROSTING

- 2⅓ cups (350 g) confectioners' (icing) sugar
- 1–2 tablespoons boiling water
- 1–2 teaspoons white rum or fruit liqueur
- 3 drops red food coloring Pistachios, marzipan roses, or candied (crystallized) violets, to decorate

1. Preheat the oven to 375°F (190°C/gas 5). Butter a 13 x 9-inch (23 x 33-cm) baking pan and line with parchment paper.

2. Sift the flour and salt into a small bowl. Beat the eggs and sugar in a double boiler over barely simmering water with an electric mixer at high speed until the mixture falls from the blades in ribbons. Use a large rubber spatula to gradually fold in the flour and butter. Pour the mixture into the prepared pan, spreading it out evenly.

3. Bake for 15–20 minutes, or until golden brown and a toothpick inserted into the center comes out clean. Cool the cake in the pan for 15 minutes.

4. Sprinkle some superfine sugar onto a large sheet of parchment paper. Turn the cake out onto the paper. Use a long sharp knife to cut the cake horizontally into three equal layers.

5. Brush the tops with apricot preserves. Place the three pieces on top of each other with a preserves layer on top.

6. Lightly dust a surface with confectioners' sugar. Roll out the marzipan to ¼ inch (3 mm) thick. Cut to fit the top layer and place it on the sandwiched cake. Cover with parchment paper and position a plate or board on top. Set aside for 5 hours, until the cake is evenly pressed into shape. Use a long sharp knife to cut into 1-inch (2.5-cm) squares.

7. To prepare the frosting, mix 1⅔ cups (250 g) of confectioners' sugar and 1–1½ tablespoons of water in a small bowl. Add the rum and stir until smooth.

8. Place the petits fours on parchment paper and drizzle frosting over them, letting it run down the sides. Set aside until the frosting has set.

9. Use the remaining confectioners' sugar, water, and food coloring to make pink frosting. Spoon it into a small freezer bag and cut off a tiny corner. Pipe whirls and lines over the petits fours. Decorate with pistachios, marzipan roses, or violets.

chocolate truffles

Serve these truffles in brightly colored mini paper cups or pile them into martini glasses and place on the table at the end of a meal.

⊚ Serves 12

◓ 15 minutes

🌡 2 hours

⏲ 3–5 minutes

🍸 1

3½ tablespoons unsalted butter, softened

⅓ cup (50 g) confectioners' (icing) sugar

⅓ cup (90 ml) heavy (double) cream

2 tablespoons vanilla sugar

12 ounces (350 g) dark chocolate, grated

4 tablespoons unsweetened cocoa powder

1. **Beat** the butter and confectioners' sugar in a medium bowl until pale and creamy.

2. **Bring** the cream to a boil in a small saucepan over medium heat. Add the vanilla sugar and stir to dissolve. Pour the hot cream into the butter mixture and stir in the chocolate. Chill for at least 2 hours.

3. **Form** the mixture into balls and roll in the cocoa. Store in the refrigerator until you are ready to serve.

If you liked this recipe, you will love these ones too:

chocolate **hedgehogs**

296

chocolate **hokey pokey**

310

chocolate **walnut** fudge

312

chocolate hokey pokey

This candy comes from New Zealand where "hokey pokey"—a kind of honeycomb toffee—is also a top-selling type of ice cream. Try making this recipe without the chocolate coating and stirring the broken pieces into vanilla ice cream.

Serves 8–10

10 minutes

Bout 1 hour

10 minutes

2

5	tablespoons (60 g) sugar
2	tablespoons corn (golden) syrup
1	teaspoon baking soda (bicarbonate of soda)
8	ounces (250 g) dark chocolate

1. **Butter** a 9-inch (23-cm) square baking pan.

2. **Combine** the sugar and corn syrup in a medium-large saucepan over low heat. Stirring constantly, bring to a gentle boil. Simmer gently for 4 minutes, stirring often.

3. **Remove** from the heat and stir in the baking soda. The mixture will bubble up, quickly doubling or tripling in volume. Working rapidly, pour into the prepared pan. Let cool to room temperature.

4. **Melt** the chocolate in a double boiler over barely simmering water. Let cool for 5 minutes.

5. **Remove** the hokey pokey from the pan and break or cut into bite-size pieces. Using tongs, dip the pieces into the chocolate, swirling to coat well. Place on a baking sheet.

6. **Let set** for at least 30 minutes before serving.

If you liked this recipe, you will love these ones too:

chocolate hedgehogs

296

chocolate truffles

308

chocolate walnut fudge

312

chocolate walnut fudge

You can speed things up considerably by placing the buttered pan in the freezer while the fudge cooks and by placing the pan with the cooked fudge in a bowl of cold water as you beat it to thicken. If preferred, leave the walnuts out.

Serves 12

10 minutes

1–2 hours

8–10 minutes

1

2 cups (400 g) sugar
½ cup (125 ml) milk
⅓ cup (90 g) salted butter, cut up
⅓ cup (50 g) unsweetened cocoa powder

1 teaspoon vanilla extract (essence)
1 cup (125 g) coarsely chopped walnuts

1. **Butter** an 8-inch (20-cm) square baking pan.

2. **Combine** the sugar, milk, butter, and cocoa powder in a medium saucepan over medium-low heat. Stir slowly and continuously as it comes to a boil. Make sure that the sugar has dissolved completely before it reaches a boil. Simmer gently for 3–4 minutes, or until it reaches the soft ball stage, 238°F (116°C) on a candy thermometer. At this temperature, if you drop a spoonful of the mixture into iced water, it will make a limp, sticky ball that flattens when you remove it from the water. Remove from the heat and let cool for 5 minutes.

3. **Add** the vanilla and walnuts and beat with a wooden spoon until thick and almost set, about 5 minutes. Pour into the prepared pan.

4. **Chill** in the refrigerator until firm, 1–2 hours. Cut into squares.

If you liked this recipe, you will love these ones too:

chocolate **hedgehogs**

296

chocolate **truffles**

308

chocolate **hokey pokey**

310

peanut brittle

A brittle is a type of very hard candy embedded with nuts, including peanuts, almond, and pecans. To vary this recipe, replace the peanuts with the same quantity of almonds or pecans.

Serves 20

20 minutes

1 hour

10 minutes

1

2	cups (400 g) sugar
1	cup (250 ml) light corn (golden) syrup
¾	cup (180 ml) water
2	cups (300 g) raw peanuts, halved
3	tablespoons unsalted butter

1. **Butter** a large baking sheet.

2. **Combine** the sugar, corn syrup, and water in a medium saucepan over low heat, stirring until the sugar dissolves. Increase the heat to medium and simmer until the mixture turns golden brown and reaches the hard-crack stage, 300°F (150°C) on a candy thermometer. At this temperature, if you drop a spoonful of the mixture into iced water, it will form stiff threads that break easily when you remove them from the water.

3. **Remove** from the heat and stir in the peanuts and butter. Beat well until thickened and almost set. Pour onto the prepared sheet, spreading quickly with a spatula to about $1/2$ inch (1 cm) thick.

4. **Let cool** to room temperature, at least 1 hour. Break or cut into bite-size pieces.

If you liked this recipe, you will love these ones too:

pecan **tartlets**

302

chocolate **hokey pokey**

310

Index

A
Apricot bread 134
Artichoke hearts stuffed with cheese 236
Asparagus & goat cheese tartlets 252

B
Baby focaccias with cream cheese & prosciutto 96
Baby focaccias with olives & pine nuts 94
Baby focaccias with tomato & prosciutto 92
Bagels with turkey, cheese & cranberry sauce 188
Baked chicken & coconut meatballs 196
Baked scallops with mushrooms & béchamel 156
Baked scallops with prosciutto 158
Beef
–Beef fajitas 190
–Classic beef burgers 192
–Steak sandwiches 194
Beet dip with toast 22
Bell peppers
–Crab cakes with roasted bell pepper sauce 166
–Eggplant & bell pepper salad 228
–Ricotta mousse with charred bell pepper sauce 226
–Roasted bell peppers with anchovies 238
Blue cheese bites 86
Bread rings 70
Brie & peach tartlets 60

C
Cheese & celery snacks 224
Cheese & tomato pinwheels 114
Cheese-filled barquettes 82
Chicken

–Baked chicken & coconut meatballs 196
–Chicken liver & orange pâté 204
–Jamaican jerk chicken wraps 186
–Sweet & spicy chicken wraps 184
–Tuscan chicken liver crostini 54
Chocolate
–Chocolate hedgehogs 296
–Chocolate hedgehogs 298
–Chocolate hokey pokey 310
–Chocolate macadamia cupcakes 294
–Chocolate spumone with pistachios 290
–Chocolate truffles 308
–Chocolate walnut fudge 312
Clams
–Clam crostini 48
–Mussels & clams 152
Classic beef burgers 192
Crab
–Crab & avocado salad 140
–Crab cakes with roasted bell pepper sauce 166
Croquettes with ham & cheese 198
Crostini with ratatouille 36

D
Deep fried okra 268
Deep fried calamari with almond crust 176

E
Easy potato knishes 242
Eggplant
–Eggplant & bell pepper salad 228
–Sicilian eggplant fritters 276

F
Fennel salad 230
Fiery meatballs 214
Filled focaccia with goat cheese 90

Filled pizzas with tomato & parmesan 106
Focaccia
–Baby focaccias with cream cheese & prosciutto 96
–Baby focaccias with olives & pine nuts 94
–Baby focaccias with tomato & prosciutto 92
–Hummus with toasted focaccia 18
–Quick gorgonzola focaccia 124
–Whole-wheat focaccia with rosemary 122
Fresh sage leaf fritters 266
Fried mozzarella 280
Fried parmesan puffs 278
Fried polenta pieces with mushroom sauce 58
Fried polenta with mushrooms, peas & cheese 56
Frosted mini almond palmiers 304

G
Garbanzo bean dip with crudités 24
Garbanzo bean flatbread 76
Garlic shrimp 160
Goat cheese & fruit salad 234
Gorgonzola & onion pizza with fresh sage 110
Grilled fish with spicy coconut chutney 162
Grilled octopus salad 142

H
Ham pâté 202
Herb mayonnaise barquettes 80
Herb rolls 120
Herb tempura 264
Hummus with toasted focaccia 18

I
Italian sausage crostini 52

J
Jamaican jerk chicken wraps 186

K
Kiwi sorbet 286

L
Lamb kebabs with tzatziki 218
Lebanese pizzas 108
Leek & almond quiche 254
Lemon tartlets 300
Liver pâté 208

M
Meatballs
–Baked chicken & coconut meatballs 196
–Fiery meatballs 214
–Meatballs with sage butter 216
–Pilotas 210
Melon sorbet with orange & basil 288
Mexican ceviche 146
Mini margarita muffins 292
Mushrooms
– Baked scallops with mushrooms & béchamel 156
–Fried polenta pieces with mushroom sauce 58
–Fried polenta with mushrooms, peas & cheese 56
–Porcini mushroom crostini 38
Mussels
–Mussels & clams 152
–Stuffed mussels 154

N

Neapolitan crêpes 246

O

Onions
–Gorgonzola & onion pizza with fresh sage 110
–Onion bhajis with yogurt dip 272
–Onion fritters with balsamic vinegar 274
–Onion, cheese & olive triangles 98
–Piquant onion pinwheels 112
–Pizzettas with caramelized onions & blue cheese 102
–Quick cheese & onion bread 130
Oregano breadsticks 72
Oysters on the half shell 150

P

Palmiers with pine nuts & parmesan 78
Pan-fried squid with lemon 174
Parmesan puffs 74
Pea & pecorino ring 244
Peanut brittle 314
Pear & hazelnut crostoni 34
Pecan tartlets 302
Petits-fours 306
Pilotas 210
Piquant onion pinwheels 112
Pizza
–Filled pizzas with tomato & parmesan 106
–Gorgonzola & onion pizza with fresh sage 110
–Lebanese pizzas 108
–Pizzettas with caramelized onions & blue cheese 102
–Pizzettas with ricotta & zucchini 104

Porcini mushroom crostini 38
Pretzels 68
Prosciutto, peach & blue cheese crostini 40
Puff pastry vegetable parcels 248

Q

Quick butternut & parmesan loaf 126
Quick cheese & onion bread 130
Quick gorgonzola focaccia 124
Quick savory loaf 132
Quick whole-wheat yogurt bread 128

R

Ratatouille tart 256
Ricotta
–Pizzettas with ricotta & zucchini 104
–Ricotta & zucchini tartlets 100
–Ricotta dip with crudités 20
–Ricotta mousse with charred bell pepper sauce 226
Roasted bell peppers with anchovies 238
Rustic pâté 206

S

Salami with fresh figs 180
Salmon carpaccio with lemon & peppercorns 148
Salmon fish cakes 170
Seafood bruschetta 50
Seafood salad 144
Shrimp
–Garlic shrimp 160
–Shrimp & papaya salad 138
–Shrimp skewers 172
–Vol-au-vents with cream sauce & shrimp 62